BIG IDEAS
for
SMALL YOUTH GROUPS

BIG IDEAS
for
SMALL YOUTH GROUPS

Patrick Angier

with

Nick Aiken

Cartoons by Dan Donovan

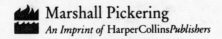

Marshall Pickering
An Imprint of HarperCollinsPublishers

Marshall Pickering is an Imprint of
HarperCollins*Religious*
Part of HarperCollins*Publishers*
77–85 Fulham Palace Road, London W6 8JB

First published in Great Britain
in 1992 by Marshall Pickering
10 9 8 7 6 5 4 3 2

A catalogue record for this book is
available from the British Library

ISBN 0 551 02168 3

Printed and bound in Great Britain by
HarperCollinsManufacturing Glasgow

Contents

Thanks

There are a number of people I would like to thank for their help in the production of this book: Beverley Steel who typed the manuscript and Nick Aiken who edited it, the Young People who participated in the Youth Groups who have tried and tested these ideas . . . for the fun we've had, the laughter we've shared and the faith we have discovered together.

I should also like to thank St George's House, Devon for the basis of Action Adventure Walk, the Surrey Association of Youth Clubs for Lost on the Moon, and St Stephen's Church for the support they give me in my ministry.

Foreword

A young writer once sent off a manuscript to a potential publisher asking for comments on his text. The senior editor wrote back with the reply, "Young man, I am pleased to say that your work is both good and original. Unfortunately the bits that are good aren't original and the bits that are original aren't good!" Though the young man didn't get the book contract he was looking for, he was actually in rather prestigous company. No less a writer than C.S. Lewis once made the claim that almost 90 per cent of all his ideas were second-hand – borrowed from the work of others.

I've been involved with Christian youth work for the last twenty years, during which time I have learnt a vital principle – "All the most original youth work ideas are borrowed ones." One of the best things about being asked to write the foreword for this book was that I was sent a complete copy of the manuscript on loose-leaf paper several months ago. That means I've already been able to use some of the ideas it contains with groups I'm involved with. When you're faced with the same group of teenagers week after week, life as a youth leader can be more than a little demanding. That's why *Big Ideas for Small Youth Groups* is such a valuable resource. In your hands is a dictionary of tried and tested, life-saving ideas just waiting for you to borrow and make use of.

But there's a second reason why I think *Big Ideas for Small Youth Groups* is such a helpful book. Even its title screams the fact at us that it's OK to be a "small youth group". As I travel around the UK, I meet lots of youth leaders doing excellent jobs with small groups, who have somehow been deceived into believing that because their group isn't "big" they are failing. Jesus chose to work with just twelve disciples. For three years he invested his time and energy into this small group of young men. If he had been the full-time youth worker at many of the churches I have known there would have been some very hard questions asked about his performance. At the end of his initial three year contract he would have probably found that it was not going to be renewed from a second term. "If he was worth his salt there should be 'something more to show for it by now' " is how the argument would run, followed by the telling comment, "I know a church, not far from here, where they've got a huge youth group."

Jesus could see beyond numbers. He looked at his group of twelve young men with all their problems, faults, mixed motives and lack of understanding, and saw their future potential. The genius of this "small group" methodology can be measured in the long-term impact they went on to make. In Acts 17:6 Jesus' followers are accused of "turning the world upside down"!

I like this book for two reasons: it's packed with "Big Ideas" and it's for "Small Youth Groups". I recommend it to you.

Steve Chalke
The Oasis Trust, London

WHAT IS A SMALL YOUTH GROUP?

A small youth group is one where the leader, or leaders have time to talk with and pastorally look after each group member in relative ease each time they gather.

A small youth group is one where the members all know each other, have shared experiences together and, as a result, know each other's strengths and weaknesses.

A small youth group, in this book, is one with between eight and 18 members. To some leaders, eight members is a dream target not yet reached, but there are resources here for the smallest of groups.

A small youth group is one where Jesus is just as much in the midst of the programme, plans and prayers as He is in a larger group.

Advantages of a small group
In a small group:
• Members can get to know everyone in the group more intimately than in a larger group. A youth group of eight members has 56 possible relationships within it. A youth group of 18 members has a possible 306 relationships in it, and a group of 30 members, 870 relationships, and so on getting vastly more complicated the larger the group is.
• Communication is easier: there are fewer people to notify of forthcoming events and therefore less chance of being left out.
• Transport is easier to arrange: a small group fits into a minibus, or into a couple of cars.
• Discipline is easier: the group is likely to be more self-regulating in behaviour and trouble makers are more easily dealt with.
• People can be open: a small group can encourage openness

1

and honesty allowing members to share problems or discoveries in their Christian faith without the intimidation a larger group creates.

● Individual members have identity: small groups have a strong group identity and loyalty. Jesus is there. Jesus' first group had only 12 members and of those there was a smaller group of only three.

How to make a small group good

1. *Prayer*. If you pray regularly for the young people in your group, they will respond to your interest and concern for them. To pray regularly for them involves finding out and knowing about their lives.

2. *The meeting place*. A small group, meeting in a large draughty hall may be very cold and intimidating, making discussion and close fellowship difficult. On the other hand, lively games and activities often need the space. If there is only a large hall, why not meet in someone's house for some evenings? Squashing into a small room is great fun. Why not involve the group in discussion about the meeting place? Look at the pros and cons and how to make it into "their place". Our Going Live group (12's to 14's), who had this problem, have just converted the redundant choir vestry into a cosy meeting room by stripping out all the old furniture, painting, decorating, putting up posters and laying a carpet. They've made it their own.

3. *Leaders*. If you are the only leader, life is easy because you know what has to be done, why it is being done, and whether or not it has been done! As soon as there is more than one leader, time will have to be spent on co-ordination and organisation. It is important that all leaders have the same aims and understanding. If not, the group will become confused and problems will develop.

4. *Pastoral care*. Whatever the number of leaders in a small group, it is possible to look after all the members with a quality

of caring that is difficult to achieve in a large group. Why not create opportunities to develop this? It is one of the real strengths of small youth groups to be able to invite members round for tea, allowing them to call in and see you (maybe one night a week), letting them babysit, help fix your car. At these informal times, as well as in the meetings and at church, a trust will develop that enables them to share problems and difficulties when they arise.

5. *Sizes*. Don't try to be a big group; plan the programme bearing in mind the group size and the fact that some people are always likely to miss the meeting for one reason or another. If the group is small, singing may not work. Don't worry, it doesn't mean that your group is less spiritual than "Happyville Community Fellowship" down the road. All too often sadly, the three choruses at the start of a youth meeting can be more akin to musical bingo than worship. When inviting speakers, musicians, organising joint events, etc., we must be realistic about our group numbers.

6. *Growth*. It's not your fault or the young people's that the group is small; a small group is not a failed large group. If you are always planning for more than can come, it can get depressing for everyone. Of course a group should want to grow – but there are other measures of growth than just numbers.

How this book can help
Every young person is completely unique. So it follows that no two youth groups are the same. Therefore, your group is not likely to react to material and ideas in the same way as St Polycarp's down the road or Bloggstown Evangelical Church up the road. Feel free to adapt, alter and change the activities to suit your group. When there are several illustrations and examples, choose ones to which your own group can relate.

Some of the material in this book, like questionnaires or instruction sheets, can be photocopied if you can enlarge them to a good size. Remember to acknowledge where it is copied from on the photocopy.

Always try wherever possible to use games and ideas with enthusiasm and imagination (even after a hard week's work!). Vary lighting and seating arrangements, and if possible match the atmosphere to the activity.

Some sessions are written out in detail, others, like the ideas montage in the Down the Pole section, are suggestions to be adapted to suit your own situation. It is best with every session to see if there are ways to adapt the material to suit your particular group. Sections within the individual sessions which call for you as leader to input your own ideas and material or facilitate the group are given the following headings:

Talk-to: Talk to the group in a way which is natural to you and with which both you and your group are comfortable. Using familiar examples and illustrations helps the group to get your message. If you do not understand what you are trying to explain, the young people will not understand either. Read the Bible passages and if you are stuck, ask your minister or pastor for any help that you need.

Briefing: Explain the instructions to the group, ensuring that everyone understands the task in hand.

De-briefing: This operates at several different levels:
What happened? Who did what? What was said, etc.
How everyone felt: did feelings change throughout the task?
Did people feel differently towards each other?
How did we react?
What can we learn: are there situations we can apply this to? etc.

Going further: An opportunity to look at the subject in a little more detail, often in the form of a more complex Bible study.

Being a youth leader is never easy. Perhaps as the leader of a small group you feel especially isolated in your task or discouraged by what you see or hear about happening elsewhere. Do not give up. Jesus never promised any of his followers an easy

4

ride or a soft option – and, quite honestly, would you want that?

Instead, as you use this book, we pray that God will increase your sense of the challenge, risk, excitement and thrill of being called to serve Him in your youth group.

ICE BREAKERS

Ice Breakers are useful for starting the evening programme in an exciting and dynamic way. For small or unmusical youth groups, they are a great alternative to singing choruses. Ice Breakers come in three "flavours": participation games, up-front games and reflective games.

Participation games
Everyone takes part and these games often involve movement and action. They can involve teams or individuals. Sometimes there are winners but there are never losers. Examples are Four Square Death Ball, Balloon Relay.

Up-front games
These are played with volunteers, chosen by whatever method is appropriate – but never against the participants' will. The volunteers are up at the front and the rest of the youth group watch . . . cheer . . . laugh . . . and also share in the experience. Examples are Sumo Knights, Worm in the Ground, Spaghetti Hairdo.

Reflective games
These often relate feelings and emotions; they can be quiet exercises in trust or involve touch. Sometimes they create opportunities for the young people to share openly and honestly about themselves. Examples are If I Were . . . , Hand to hand, More Fat Than Thin.

Sumo knights

Aim

A lively opener which the lads will love as participants and the girls as spectators. (or vice versa!)

Numbers

4 or more

Equipment

Chalk and a suitable floor.

Preparation

Draw a 15-foot diameter circle on the floor with the chalk.

How to play

1. The players need to be in pairs. Two pairs mount up piggy-back style and enter the circle. Each pair salutes the opposition by bowing "sumo style".

2. The object is either to knock over the opposition, thus scoring two points, or to knock them out of the circle, scoring one point. If either pair puts a foot outside the circle, the opposition wins a bonus point.

3. The first pair to get four points is the winner.

4. The contest ends with a ceremonial bow.

Hints

Don't let either of the pairs "charge" their opposition, as this can be dangerous. It is advisable for any member wearing glasses to take them off.

Variations

1. Team Sumo. Divide the group into two equal teams and everyone has to do battle twice only. The team winning the most contests is the winner.

2. Tag Sumo. As above, except the pair in the circle can tag another pair from their team waiting on the edge of the circle and then swap over. This gives a continuous battle as in tag wrestling.

Pyramid games

Aim

Pure fun which creates a sense of working together.

Numbers

12 or more.

Preparation

None.

Equipment

None.

How to play

1. Divide the group into two teams.

2. The task is for each team to form a pyramid. Three team members on all fours make up the base, two on all fours on top of the base make the middle, and the last member makes the top.

3. Do not worry if there are any young people left over as the team has to rearrange the pyramid line-up after each of the following tasks has been completed. This ensures everyone gets a go.

4. Tasks:
    a. Turn the whole pyramid through 180°.

b. Middle layer turn about without the top layer falling off!
c. Middle person of the base turn around.
d. Ends of the base turn around.
e. Person on the top attempts to do a handstand (you may have to catch them at this point!).
f. Fastest pyramid to "sprint" the length of the hall.
g. *Ad lib* to exhaustion.

5. As each task is successfully completed, the team wins a point (except for task e. when the team gets 50!) The pyramid with the most points wins.

Variations

If you have a group of between 6 and 12 young people, then perform the tasks non-competitively, getting everyone not directly involved to encourage those who are.

Hints

Watch out for when the pyramid collapses to ensure that no one gets hurt. There may be a few bruises. Our young people moaned about the bruises, but raved about the game!

Spaghetti links

Aim

Team work, warm-up exercise.

Equipment

1 packet spaghetti (not the wholewheat variety).

Preparation

Partially cook the spaghetti.

How to play

1.   Divide the group into equal teams of between two and four members.

2.   Give each team a bowl of the partially cooked spaghetti.

3.   Each team has two minutes to construct the longest length of spaghetti string (made by tying the spaghetti lengths together).

4.   The winners will be those with the longest length lifted off the ground by the ends, without it breaking.

Hints

The cooking time of the spaghetti is crucial for the desired effect. Have a few practice goes with individual strands before cooking it all.

Four square death ball

Aim

A fast moving ice breaker.

Numbers

8 or more.

Equipment

Chalk and a football or sorbo sponge ball.

Preparation

Chalk out a square court divided into four smaller courts (each 3m × 3m).

How to play

1. Divide the group into four teams and allocate each a square. Instruct them that no one is allowed outside his or her square.

2. The object is to eliminate the opposition by hitting them on or below the knee with the ball.

3. When a player is out, he or she leaves the court.

4. If the ball goes out of play, it is returned to the last occupied court that it passed through.

5. The last team remaining is, of course, the winner.

Hints

Avoid hard balls when using this game with older teens. They can hurt if a throw is misdirected.

Ident-a-knee parade

Aim

A cringingly, ticklingly funny get-to-know-you game.

Numbers

10 or more.

Preparation

None.

Equipment

Paper and pens, blindfolds.

How to play

1.   Ask for three volunteers, who are then escorted outside to a place where they cannot hear or see anything happening inside.

2.   Ask for a further three volunteers. These have to roll up their trousers to just above the knee and stand in line as at a "knobbly knees" competition.

3.   The three people from outside are brought back into the room blindfolded, one at a time. They then have to feel the knees of the identity parade line-up and then are led outside to write down their guess at the identity of the "knees" owners.

4.   The person who guesses the most right wins a prize.

Variations

Feel feet and faces and well as or instead of knees.

Quacking ducks

Aim

Warm-up.

Numbers

10 or more.

Equipment

20 to 30 wrapped sweets or mini bars, 2 cardboard boxes to act as "bases".

Preparation

Hide the sweets around the meeting place.

How to play

1.   Divide the group into teams of equal numbers.

2.   If the teams are of less than six members, give one person the identity of "fox" and the rest "ducks". If numbers in each team are more than six, have two foxes in each team.

3.   The task of the ducks is to seek out the hidden sweets. When they find one, they have to flap their arms, jump up and down and make lots of quacking noises to inform the fox of their discovery.

4.   The fox's task is to collect the sweets found by its team and take them back to base.

5.   The winning team is the one with the most sweets.

Rules

1.   Foxes can only carry one sweet at a time.

2.   A fox can only gather sweets found by quacking ducks from his/her team.

3.   Sweets cannot be removed from base camp.

Variations

Change the animals to gorillas, lions, etc.

Hints

The more vividly the leader demonstrates the quacking and actions of a duck, the funnier the game will be.

Knight riders

Aim

Summer starter, best played outdoors.

Equipment

String, small balloons filled with water.

Preparation

Fill the balloons with water and tie a length of string to the end.

How to play

1.   Everyone finds a partner and mounts up "piggy-back" style to mimic a knight and his horse. The knight is given a balloon on a length of string.

2.   The object is to "kill" other knights by hitting them with the water balloon so that it bursts on the opposing pair.

3.   When a pair are wet, they are eliminated from the contest and the victor of the joust commandeers their water balloon and uses it to continue battle.

4.   If both balloons are burst simultaneously, both pairs are out.

5.   The pair that remains at the end are the winners.

Hints

The amount of water in the balloons and their size are important. They should not be too heavy or the string too long. Do not let the contestants hit each other in the face with the balloons as they can sting when they burst.

Variations

If the group is large, this could become a team game.

Body walk

Aim

Team work.

Equipment

Chalk.

Preparation

Draw two parallel lines across your hall, 20 feet apart.

How to play

1. Divide the group into equal sized teams of 4, 5, or 6 depending on your group size.

2. The object is to cross over the area marked by the chalk and keep the team united as a unit, i.e. holding on to each other with an allocated number of limbs touching the floor.

3. Begin with easier combinations, gradually becoming more complicated:
> 6 feet only
> 5 feet and 2 elbows
> 5 feet and 1 hand
> 4 feet and 3 hands
> 3 feet and 5 hands
> 3 feet, 4 hands, 2 elbows and 1 nose

4. Have six to ten different combinations and allocate points for each successful crossing. The team with most points wins.

More fat than thin

Aim

Thought-provoking warm-up.

Equipment

None.

Preparation

Construct a list as below.

How to play

1. Everyone stands in the middle and the leader asks, "Are you more happy than sad?" and points to one end of the room which is then designated – "sad" and then to the other end which is designated "happy".

2. The young people then have to choose which end it would be most appropriate for them to stand, and then move. There is no standing in the middle.

3. Then call another pair of characteristics, e.g. more fat than thin, and again they have to decide and move to one end of the room.
Other calls could include:
    loner/crowd seeker
    quiet/noisy
    beautiful/ugly
    extrovert/introvert

21

thinker/doer
local/foreign
Christian/Non-Christian

4. When the young people have got the hang of it, allow members to challenge other people's positions, e.g. "You're not fat," "You should be at this end," etc.

5. End with discussion, asking if people were surprised at how others perceived them.

M & M relay

Aim

Team work relay.

Numbers

6 or more.

Equipment

1 packet peanut M & M (sweets), teaspoons (enough for one each) four saucers.

Preparation

None.

How to play

1.   Divide the group into two equal teams and give everyone a teaspoon.

2.   Line up the teams in single file at one end of the hall, in line with a saucer on the floor at the other end and with a second saucer on the floor behind them.

3.   In the saucers at the far end of the hall place as many M & M's as there are team members. If the teams are small and you want a longer race, put in double the number.

4.   The player at the back of the team line runs past the team, puts the teaspoon in his or her mouth, picks up an M & M and

returns to the front of the team, carrying the M & M in the spoon.

5.   The M & M is then passed down the team from teaspoon to teaspoon (no hands allowed!). When the M & M reaches the back of the line, the last player deposits it in the saucer behind them and then runs to the end of the hall to fetch another.

6.   This continues until all the M & M's have been rescued into the saucer at the back of the team.

7.   The first team to finish is the winner.

8.   When an M & M is dropped the team have to start again (from the beginning of that round).

Y-fronts and boxer shorts

Aim

Embarrassing fun for a weekend away.

Equipment

Washing line, pegs, small cards with numbers 1 to 6 written on them, pencils, paper, prize.

Preparation

Get two of your more extrovert girls to organise a raid on the boys' dormitory – while they are out, of course – and remove half a dozen pairs of the boys' underwear (preferably clean!).

How to play

1. String a washing line across the meeting room and hang the items on it, each with a numbered card attached.

2. Choose a few girls (the shyer and quieter the better). Give them each a piece of paper and ask them to write down the boy they think each item belongs to.

3. Collect the papers and ask the owner of each pair of undies to stand up in turn.

4. The girl who makes the most correct guesses wins a prize – a pair of boxer shorts, maybe.

Variation

It has not been unknown for the boys to want the game the other way around!

Disclaimer

This game was thought up by members of our youth group!

Guzzler's relay

Aim

Ice breaker and discussion starter on greed or deception.

Equipment

2 onions, 2 mini Mars bars, 2 bananas, 2 carrots, 2 pieces of celery, 1 packet of Polos, 2 marshmallows, etc . . . some paper bags and string.

Preparation

Cut the string into enough two-foot lengths for each person to have one each. Make a small hole in the bottom of each paper bag and thread one end of the string through from the inside and tie the other end to one of the food items so that, when you hold the threaded end up, the bag will slide down the string and cover the food item. Hang a row of these bags from the ceiling, or under tables, or from strings hanging across the room.

How to play

1. Two teams line up at one end of the hall.

2. Player 1 runs to the first bag and, using teeth only, rips it away and has to eat the contents (not the wrappers or the banana skins). He or she then runs back to the team and tags the next player.

3. Because the food is in bags, they don't see what they have to eat until they have pulled off the paper.

4. The first team to have eaten everything wins.

Babies in the bath

Aim

Fun starter, team work.

Numbers

4 or more.

Equipment

1 baby bath or paddling pool, bubble bath (children's which is non-stingy), table tennis balls, 1 fork per team member, a watch.

Preparation

Fill the baby bath with water and bubble bath so that it is good and frothy (really bubbly) and put into it as many table tennis balls as you can beg, borrow or find.

How to play

1.   Divide the group into two teams and either take it in turns to play the game or use two baths.

2.   The task of the team is to get as many table tennis balls out of the bath in two minutes as they can, using forks only. Any team using hands has points deducted.

3.   If a team gets all the table tennis balls out, judging is done on the length of time taken. Otherwise, count the number of table tennis balls.

Hints

Unless the team cooperates, it is very difficult to remove the tennis balls from the bath.

Variations

Have one pool and balls of two different colours, and get both teams to play at once. The first team to remove all the balls of their colour wins.

Wet and run

Aim

A fun discussion starter.

Equipment

1 chair per player, 2 water pistols.

Preparation

Lay out the chairs in a large circle.

How to play

1.   Everyone sits on a chair apart from one member of the group who stands in the middle of the circle.

2.   Give a water pistol to the person in the middle of the circle, and place the other on an empty chair beside him in the middle of the circle.

3.   Player A (in the middle) then walks around the outside of the circle until he chooses a suitable victim (B) and shoots him or her in the back of the neck with the water pistol.

4.   After shooting B, A has to try and return to his or her chair in the middle of the circle before being shot by B, weaving in and out of the large circle of chairs.

5.   B, meanwhile, has to run to the middle of the circle, grab the water pistol off the empty chair and run around the outside of the circle.

6. If B catches A by squirting him, then B takes over in the middle of the circle. If A is not caught then he stays in the middle and the game restarts.

Hints

Do not allow any "shooting back", i.e. players are not allowed to shoot the person who shot them. The more powerful the water pistols, the better. The chair spacing needs to be varied with the group size so that the contest is fair.

This activity can be used as a discussion starter on fear, betrayal, etc.

Worm chew

Aim

Fun, warm-up.

Equipment

Red and black liquorice bootlaces.

Preparation

Tie four bootlaces together to make a string. You need one string for each couple.

How to play

1.   Divide the group into pairs. (Do this using a game such as Balloon Pass Out, or by choosing the most appropriate or inappropriate pairs.)

2.   Everyone stands in a circle facing the centre and opposite their partner.

3.   The strings of liquorice are then stretched across the circle from partner to partner.

4.   On the command GO, the players (without using their hands) have to eat their string, eating their way towards each other and into the circle. They will become bunched up together in the middle.

5.   The first pair to eat up all of their string is the winner.

Variations

Length of string, type and colour of liquorice can all be varied. With small groups, perhaps obstacles could be added. Or if you want a screaming alternative, why not blindfold? The possibilities are endless.

Broom relay

Aim

A fun relay.

Equipment

2 brooms, 2 chairs, 2 plastic beakers, and several jugs of water.

Preparation

Lay out the course as below.

How to play

1.   Divide the group into two equal teams of any number.

2.   The two teams line up parallel to each other at one end of the hall. Half way down the hall place a broom in line with each team. At the far end put a plastic beaker full of water placed on a chair (again one for each team).

3.   The first player from each team hops down the hall to the chair at the far end and drinks the water from the beaker. He or she then hops around the chair and back to the broom. Holding the broom upright with both hands, with forehead pressed against the end of the handle he or she runs around the broom 10 times whilst keeping the brush end rotating in the same position on the floor. The player then hops back to the rest of the team.

4.   When the first player has completed the course the second player can start and so on for the rest of the team. The leader keeps the cups filled with water.

5.   The first team to finish is the winner.

Hint

Vary the number of times that the young people run around the broom according to age and the number of goes they are having.

Variations

Add a task after running around the broom, such as blowing up a balloon or stacking five wooden toy blocks on top of each other.

Balloon animals

Aim

This fun variation on an old game is a great way to divide the group into pairs or teams.

Equipment

For each person, 1 balloon and 1 piece of paper.

Preparation

Decide whether you want the group divided into pairs, threes, fours, etc., and write an animal's name on that number of pieces of paper. If you want the group in teams of four, for example, write "dog" on four pieces of paper, "duck-billed platypus" on four, etc. Each piece of paper needs to be folded and placed in a balloon which is then blown up and tied.

How to play

1.   At the start of the evening, pass out the balloons. They all burst their balloons by sitting on them or hugging them against someone else (in silence).

2.   When they have done this, they need to retrieve the piece of paper without showing anyone what is written on it.

3.   They now find the other members of their team by wandering around and making their animal's noise or action.

Trumps

Aim

An old favourite to get them moving.

Numbers

From 4 to 400!

Equipment

Pack of cards, one chair per person.

How to play

1. Everyone sits on chairs in a circle.

2. Each person is given a playing card and they must note from this, what suit they are for the rest of the game (hearts, clubs, diamonds or spades). The cards are then taken back in and the leader shuffles the pack.

3. The leader turns over the top card and calls out the suit. Everyone whose card was that suit moves one seat to the right and if there is someone there already, sits on their knee.

4. Another card is turned and those with that suit move one seat to their right, unless they are being sat on, in which case they are unable to move.

5. The leader continues to call out suits quite quickly.

6. The winner is the first person to move all the way around the circle and return to his or her original seat (even if there is a pile already on it!).

Variations

1. If the group is very small, have several laps.

2. Try having the red suits moving anti-clockwise and the blacks clockwise, just to complicate matters.

Worm in the ground, or Snake in the Bog

Aim

A screaming start to the evening.

Equipment

Liquorice strings, of the same or of differing lengths. 4 bowls of chocolate instant whip (or use just one bowl).

Preparation

Place the liquorice strings in the bottom of the bowl leaving one end of the string visible over the edge, and pour in the runny instant whip.

How to play

1. Choose four volunteers either by encouragement or bribery!

2. Explain that the first person to eat the liquorice string will win a prize, be a Mega Star for the evening, etc.

3. The contestants position themselves next to an end of liquorice string and on the command "Go", start chewing the string without using their hands.

4. The winner is the first person to eat the string.

Hints

1.   If your group meets in your lounge, it might be a good idea to protect the carpet with a plastic sheet.

2.   The consistency of the instant whip must not be too solid or too runny.

Variations

Blindfold the contestants and use differing lengths of liquorice. With lots of cheering and group noise, the last contestant will not realize that he or she is chewing away alone. Use as a discussion starter on deception or being the odd one out.

Balloon relay

Aim

Fun, warm-up.

Equipment

Balloons (long, thin ones).

Preparation

Blow up the balloons.

How to play

1.   Divide the group into teams of between 4 and 6.

2.   The teams line up one member behind another at one end of the hall.

3.   The first person in each team places the balloon between the knees and hops down the hall, round a chair placed at the far end and back to the team.

4.   He or she then passes the balloon to the next person in the line without using their hands.

5.   Player 2 then hops around the course with the balloon between the knees and passes it on to player 3.

6.   The winning team is the first to have all players complete the course.

7. Any who use their hands or let the balloon touch the floor have to start again.

Variations

1. Add a balloon each time the team completes a round. e.g. one under the chin, one under each arm, etc.

2. Play the game blindfolded.

Can I help?

Aim

A quiet warm-up.

Equipment

Problem cards.

Preparation

Write out problem cards, for example:

1. Your are an old person whose garden is overgrown now that your husband is dead.

2. Your boyfriend has packed you in.

3. You have been sacked from your Saturday job.

4. You want to give up smoking.

5. You are lonely.

6. Your parents do not like your friends.

7. (Add your own.)

How to play

1. One person draws a card. The rest of the group has to ask questions to find out what the problem is.

2. Questions can only be answered "yes" or "no".

3. Each person is allowed a maximum of three questions, and then one guess at what the problem is.

4. Individuals score one point per problem guessed correctly.

Polo mint pass

Aim

Fun, warm-up.

Equipment

2 packets of Polos, cocktail sticks.

How to play

1. Divide into two teams and give each person a cocktail stick.

2. Put an equal number of Polos on two chairs at the end of the hall.

3. Player one runs to the chair, puts the cocktail stick into his or her mouth and then, without using hands, picks up a Polo.

4. Players then return to their team and pass the Polo from cocktail stick to cocktail stick down the line (the sticks always being in players' mouths) without using their hands. The last player drops the Polo from the stick into a bowl and runs to the other end of the hall to pick another Polo off the chair.

5. The first team to have all their Polos in the bowl is the winner.

Variation

Introduce some obstacles for the Polo carriers to climb over or under.

Balloon gladiators

Aim

Warm-up.

Equipment

Balloons, string.

How to play

1. Divide into equal teams.

2. The teams sit facing each other on a row of chairs and number off in pairs from left to right (starting from 1).

3. Each person is given a balloon and piece of string. They blow the balloon up and tie it to the ankle with string.

4. A number is called out. The two people with that number must try to burst each other's balloon by stamping on it, at the same time protecting their own balloon from being burst.

5. The team gets a point for each surviving balloon. The team with the most points wins.

Variations

1. Call more than one number at once.

2. Have replacement balloons and string so that players may have more than one go.

3. Make the two gladiators hold either end of a rope loop in their left hands so that they are unable to run away from each other.

If I were . . .

Aim

A non-competitive discussion starter.

Equipment

None.

Preparation

None.

Action

1. Set up the room so that the seats are facing each other and a friendly atmosphere is created to encourage sharing.

2. Name a category, e.g. Animal.

3. In turns, everyone says, "If I were an animal, I would be a . . ." If they wish they can explain the reason for their choice.

4. Everyone should be quiet while people speak, but may ask questions when they have finished.

Variations

Use any number of categories: flowers, trees, houses, shops, people, etc.

Hints

Try to ensure that people share what they *are* like and not what they would *want* to be like. Or you may decide to do both together: "If I were an animal, I would be . . ." and "If I were an animal, I would like to be . . ."

Hand to hand

Aim

Non-competitive warm-up.

Equipment

None.

Preparation

None.

How to play

1. Everyone needs to be in pairs. If there is a young person without a partner, partner them yourself, or partner them with another leader so that no one is left out.

2. Call out a selection of touching positions, e.g. sole to sole, heel to heel, etc. Each pair carries out the command e.g. they sit on the floor with the soles of their feet touching. Suggestions for positions:

    Hand to hand   Nose to nose
    Back to back   Palm to palm
    Elbow to elbow   Head to head
    Knee to knee   Ear to ear
    "Backside" to "backside"

3. After a while ask everyone to swap partners.

Hints

This game is best played in a mellow atmosphere so that people do not feel too self-conscious. Do not play after energetic or funny ice breakers. It is a relaxing, gentle way to prepare for the evening's activity.

Pie plate game

Aim

This game doesn't really have an aim, but the youth group will love it . . . except those who lose.

Equipment

Five plates of custard pie foam, tape player and "trendy" music.

Preparation

Assemble the equipment and make up the custard pies.

How to play

1.   Persuade 5 volunteers to come forward and play the game. (Suggest nominations, offer prizes, etc.)

2.   Stand the volunteers at the front – on the stage, or somewhere where people can see.

3.   Player 1 is given a custard pie plate. When the music begins he or she passes it down the line to the next person who does the same and so on up and down the line for as long as the music plays.

4.   When the music stops, the person who is holding the plate can "custard pie" the person who passed the plate on to him.

5.   The "pied" person is eliminated and the game continues (and the suspense grows) until there is only one person left.

Hint

Those standing in the middle of the line are more likely to lose than those at the ends.

Spaghetti hairdo

Aim

Up front ice breaker.

Equipment

3 chairs, 3 bowls, cooked spaghetti.

Preparation

Cook the spaghetti.

How to play

1. Ask for three male volunteers and ask them to come and sit down on the chairs.

2. Explain that none of the lads has a trendy hairdo and that you would like three girls to come and restyle their hair.

3. When the girls are in place, bring out the bowls of spaghetti and explain that the girls have to restyle the lads' hair (putting the spaghetti actually on the lads' heads).

4. Give them three minutes to construct a hairstyle and get the rest of the group to judge the winner.

5. Give the winner a prize (hair gel?).

FAITHBUILDERS

The sessions in this section are aimed at building up the young people's spiritual lives and giving them teaching on the Christian faith and Christian life.

Faithbuilding is what it is all about. Like teaching a child to walk, we need to encourage our young people one step at a time. The process will move them on from their first contact to their discovering who Jesus is, what the Gospel is all about, through conversion and filling with the Holy Spirit and into growth, service and action.

Each step of the way, they need our encouragement and prayer. The teenage faith journey, although step by step, is not a gentle hill climb. It is more often a series of steep climbs and plummeting descents as their emotions swing from one extreme to another. As we walk with them, picking them up when they are down and living with the enthusiasm of the "ups", the faithbuilding process can be seen.

Faithbuilding is *hard work*! We live in a world that is in enemy hands. The Apostle Paul said, "We battle not against flesh and blood but against the principalities and powers; the rulers of this dark age." Faithbuilding cannot be done in our own strength. We need to trust and rely on Jesus and be constantly filled with the Holy Spirit.

"Now to Him who is able to do immeasurably more than all we ask or imagine, according to his power at work within us, to him be glory in the Church and in Christ Jesus throughout all generations, for ever and ever. Amen."

The real thing

Aim

To investigate what a Christian is.

Equipment

A can of Coka Cola, 1 can of Pepsi, 2 plates, plastic cups, sliced bread, margarine, butter. Labels, cards, pencils, paper, icing equipment, 1 empty box and a cake, either home-made or bought. (We used a sugar lump box and a bought sponge cake, then trimmed it to the same size and shape as the box.)

Preparation

1.   Label two sets of cups A and B and the plates C and D.

2.   Set up the icing equipment in another room or in the kitchen away from the rest.

3.   Prepare cards (see below).

Warm-up

1.   Give each person a paper and pencil.

2.   Pour a little Coke into one set of cups and Pepsi into the other. Ensure that no one know which is which.

3.   Spread some pieces of bread with butter, cut them into small pieces and put on a plate. Do the same with the margarine and set those pieces on a separate plate.

4. Run a tasting competition. Everyone has to identify which is which and write the answers down.

5. When they have all made their choice, let them know which was Coke and which was Pepsi, and which was butter and which margarine. Identify the young people who guessed correctly.

Talk-to

"One of the problems we face as followers of Jesus is knowing whether someone is a Christian or not. We may even doubt sometimes if we are. Today we are investigating the real thing. Can we tell what it is to be a Christian or is it as indistinguishable as Coke and Pepsi? To do this we need two volunteers."

Action

1. Give volunteers the icing instruction card and send them off to the kitchen.

Icing instruction card
1. You should have the following equipment: icing sugar, food colouring, water, butter/margarine (left over from earlier), bowls, spoons, knives, forks, a cake and a box.
2. Your task is to decorate the cake and the box with icing so that the rest of the group will not be able to tell which is which.
3. After approximately 20 minutes the two "cakes" need to be ready.
4. Bring the real cake in on a white plate and the other on a coloured plate.

2. Divide the remaining group into teams of four and give each team a character card. From the information on the card, they have to assess whether or not the character described is a Christian.

Character cards

JOHN JONES
Age 43.
Occupation Builder.
Hobbies Darts; plays for the local pub team.
Married, has two teenage children, both at school. Wife is a secretary. Fought for his country in the Falklands.

PHILIP LEWIS
Age 22.
Student at London University, studying Genetics.
Unmarried, has steady girlfriend.
Hobbies include skiing, mountain climbing.

HELEN SMITH
Age 57.
Works as a manageress of the local Charity Shop, was formerly a nurse in Africa.
Unmarried, no children.
Hobbies local Women's Institute and Bridge Club.

RACHEL WEST
Age 27.
Unemployed, helps at volunteer bureau.
Unmarried, with one child, James aged 6.
Hobbies reading when there is time.

3. Ask each group to report back on why the person on the card might or might not be a Christian. Two people from the group write down onto large sheets of paper the reasons why they might or might not be. If groups say they do not know, ask them to find indications why each of the characters might or might not be.

4. At this point get the two "iced cakes" brought in. Those who have made them must keep quiet and are not permitted to participate in the next stage. (Send them back into the kitchen to wash up!)

5. Let the group have a good look at the two cakes and ask them which they would like a slice of.

6. Count up the number of people who would like a slice of the cake on the white plate, divide the cake and dish out the slices.

7. Make a slow job of counting how many would like a slice

of the other cake so that those with cake can eat it. Then Cut up the iced box and give out pieces.

8.   Bring back the cake icers from the kitchen.

De-brief

1.   How did you feel when the cardboard cake was cut? Ask those who had a cake, then those who had none.

2.   Why did people choose the cardboard cake?

3.   What dangers are there in judging by the outside?

Talk-to

One of the biggest mistakes people make about Christianity is assuming that a Christian is someone who is good on the outside and does all the right things. Jesus had to deal with religious people who were good on the outside but He said they were like "whitewashed tombs", i.e. all clean on the outside, but full of death and rot on the inside. So, if a Christian is not a "good person", what is a Christian?

A Christian is someone who has taken four simple steps:

A = ADMIT. A Christian has admitted that he has rebelled against God and gone his own way and needs to turn away from selfishness and sin and turn back to God.

B = BELIEVE. A Christian believes (puts all his trust – like making a 'bungee jump'*) that Jesus, in dying on the Cross, took our sins away and then by rising from the dead brings new and eternal life.

C = COUNT THE COST. A Christian has counted the cost of Jesus being Lord of all. Unless Jesus is Lord, He

---

* Bungee Jump: the dangerous sport of jumping off bridges held only by a stretchable bungee rope. The jumper has to have total faith in the rope, the harness and the fastenings.

cannot be Saviour. He is Lord of all the areas of our lives: relationships, money, etc . . .

D = DO. A Christian is someone who has done something! Christians have asked God the Holy Spirit into their life, to empower them to live our the Christian life.

If appropriate, end with an opportunity for the young people to make a commitment or recommitment of their lives to God.

Is God green?

Aim

To investigate environmental issues from a Christian perspective.

Preparation

Prepare the quiz, Bible investigation and problem page sheets.

Equipment

Bibles, pencils, pens, photocopied sheets.

Warm-up

1. Hand out copies of the Green Quiz, and ask each member to fill one in (see p. 67).

2. Get them to mark their papers.
    1. a=5 b=1 c=−5 (minus)   6. a=0 b=0 c=0
    2. a=5 b=0 c=−5 (minus)   7. a=0 b=5 c=2
    3. a=5 b=2 c=−5 (minus)   8. a=5 b=2 c=0
    4. a=5 b=2 c=0   9. a=5 b=2 c=0
    5. a=5 b=2 c=−5 d=0   10. a=5 b=2 c=0

3. Compare results.
40 to 50	A real greeny!
20 to 40	Could do better (Greenish)
0 to 20	Need to do better (Not really green)
−20 to 0	Maybe it's time to start (What's a Green?)

Main session

1. Divide them into groups of four and give each group the sheet of Bible investigation questions.

   Bible investigation
   Genesis 1:26–30
   Mark 6:16
   Luke 12:27–31
   Psalms 24:1–2

2. Ask them to read the Bible passages.

3. Ask each group to discuss these questions:
   Does God reveal himself in creation?
   What is man's position in creation and what is his responsibility for it?
   How did Jesus say we should look at creation?

4. After about 20 minutes, ask the small groups to report back to the whole group.

5. Now return to groups of four. Give everyone a problem page sheet (see p. 68)

6. Each group has 15 minutes to prepare their answers to the problem pages.

7. Gather everyone together and share the letters and the answers.

8. Sum up and include, if appropriate, comments on following points. Christianity does have something to say on environmental issues. As Christians, we should get involved rather than staying on the sidelines.

9. Close with prayer.

Green Quiz

1. If you use cosmetics, do you use ones that have not been tested on animals?

    a. always   b. sometimes   c. never

2. If you use a car, does it run on unleaded petrol!?

    a. yes   b. no   c. don't know

3. Do you walk or cycle to youth group rather than drive or get a lift?

    a. yes   b. no   c. occasionally

4. Do you use recycled paper to save trees?

    a. always   b. occasionally   c. never

5. If you use deodorant, do you use ozone-friendly brands?

    a. always   b. occasionally   c. never
    d. What's deodorant?

6. Do you save energy by sleeping in at weekends?

    a. always   b. sometimes   c. never

7. When leaving a room, do you switch off the lights?

    a. never   b. always   c. sometimes

8. Do you take your newspapers to collection points to be re-cycled?

    a. always   b. sometimes   c. never

9. Do you take glass to the bottle bank?

    a. always   b. sometimes   c. never

10. Do you buy clothes from charity shops, recycled?

    a. always   b. sometimes   c. never

Problem page sheet (Group A)

You are a problem page editor for a new teenage magazine for Christians. How would you answer the following questions?

1.   What can I do? I want to become a vegetarian but my parents tell me I will not get the right vitamins and insist that I eat a roast Sunday lunch.

2.   My R.E. teacher at school told us that Christianity is a religion of environmental exploitation. Is this true?

3.   We live next to a hospital and the incinerator always smells horrible at night but in the day time is O.K. Twice this term I have had to take time off school with a chest infection. What can I do?

Problem page sheet (Group B)

You are a problem page editor for a new teenage magazine for Christians. How would you answer the following questions:

1.   I have just passed my driving test and can only afford an old car. Is it true that older cars cannot run on lead free petrol? What should I do?

2.   I'm 17 and keen on getting involved in my community as a Christian. The town has no bottle bank. How can I arrange to start one at church?

3.   What does Paul mean in 1 Corinthians 8:13 when he says: "If what I eat causes my brother to fall into sin, I will never eat meat again"?

Problem page sheet (Group C)

You are the problem page editor for a new teenage magazine for Christians. How would you answer the following questions:

1.   My Mum says she can't afford to buy organically grown fruit and vegetables. I am really worried that I will get cancer from the pesticides on normal fruit and veg.

2. Is it right for a Christian to eat beefburgers from our local fast good take-away?

3. I feel that God is calling me to be a vet but it is true that in A-level Biology I will have to dissect animals that have been cruelly reared and murdered?

Talking sense

Aim

For young people one of the biggest blocks to responding to the Gospel is the language in which we disguise it. A survey of inner-city youngsters gave these definitions of various Christian words.

Abundant	A hair style; flags across the street.
Consecrate	They do it to coconuts: to make something thick.
Salvation	Collecting silver paper; rubbish collecting; helping poor people.
Doctrine	Medicine; something to do with Trade Unions.

In this session we will be looking at how we use exclusive language and how it is a barrier to our young people "reaching their friends with the Gospel of salvation".

Equipment

Magazines (N.M.E., Just 17, Skateboard, etc.), pencils, paper, some examples of prayers, creeds etc.

Preparation

Copy out questions, word match sheet, definitions.

Warm-up

1. Get the group to match words to definitions. Put up 26 definitions on the walls, each labelled with an identifying letter.

Give each person a word match sheet listing 15 words. In the space provided, they need to write in what they think the correct definitions are. (Alternatively, ask them to write their own definitions.)

Word match sheet

Word	*Definition*
1. Led to	....
2. Quiet time	....
3. A word	....
4. Blessing	....
5. Housegroup	....
6. Confession	....
7. Share	....
8. Just	....
9. Ministry	....
10. Walking in light	....
11. Living in faith	....
12. Name and claim	....
13. Charismatic	....
14. Worship time	....
15. PBST (Personal Bible Study Time)	....

Main session

1. Divide the group into small groups of three or four and give each group a magazine to examine and an action card.

Action card
1. Divide the magazine pages between your group.
2. Read carefully, and whenever you find an "in word", write it down.
3. Compile a list of these words.

2. After the groups have compiled their lists, give them the set of questions.

Questions
1. Why were the words unknown to you?
2. What effect does "in language" have on:
   – those who do not know what it means?
   – those who do know what it means?
3. Are these effects good, or bad?

3. Draw the groups back together and ask them to report back on their investigations and read out their answers.

4. Divide into small groups. Give each group a Scripture passage (e.g. Romans 3:23–24), creed or Christian prayer and ask them to repeat the exercise, listing the words and then writing their answers to the questions.

5. Draw the groups back together to share their answers.

6. List the words that are a problem and ask volunteers to explain them in everyday language or using everyday examples.

7. Sum up and close, or . . .

Going further

1. Divide into pairs. One person shares his or her faith and the other plays a non-Christian, interested in knowing more. Those sharing their faith try to do so without using any of the "in words".

2. Swap over and let the other person have a go.

Parents

Aim

To help Teenagers understand the pressures and problems facing their parents, and to encourage a biblical perspective on parenting.

Equipment

Bibles, pencils, paper.

Preparation

Write out lists of Bible passages.

Main session

1. Think of your Mum and Dad. Choose a pop song which best represents each of them. (If a person has only a Mum, only a Dad or neither of these, be aware of this. They can do the exercise for one parent, step-parent or guardian. Make sure the young person does not feel excluded or uncomfortable.)

2. Now think of the car, tree or flower which best represents each parent.

3. In groups of three, share your answers.

4. Gather everyone together again and invite anyone who would like to, to share their answers with the whole group.

5. Now do the exercise in reverse. How would you parents describe you in terms of a pop song? When everyone has had

time to think about this, share the answers in small groups. (Anyone feeling particularly brave can sing it!)

6. Now introduce the *Position on the Line exercise*. Label one end of the room A, and the opposite end B. Draw a real or imaginary line from A to B. For each of the statements, the young people need to position themselves at the point on the line nearest the statement with which they agree. For each statement, give the opportunity to challenge where people are standing and encourage explanation of positioning.

Parents only act out of love	Parents only act our of self-interest.
Young people need more freedom than most parents give.	Parents need to be strict on their teenagers.
Parents don't know what it is like to be a teenager, they don't understand	Parents remember what it was like to be a teenager and understand too much.
If you were your parents, you would make a better job of parenting.	If you were your parents, you would make a worse job of parenting.

Talk-to

1. We all have different ideas on how parents should behave and what the ideal parent is like. God is the perfect parent and the Bible contains a number of guidelines for good parent-child relationships.

2. Hand our pieces of paper listing these Bible passages:

Exodus 20:12	Proverbs 29:15
Proverbs 10:1	Colossians 3:20–22
Proverbs 23:22–25	Ephesians 6:1–2

3. Ask the group to read the passages to find God's advice for parents and children.

72

4. Share the answers to the Bible study and sum up.

Going further

Get the group into pairs and give each pair a sheet listing youth and parents problems (see p. 76). Ask them to work out a role play for each situation. Then choose two or three of the role plays to be acted out in front of the group.

Discussion

How can we put the teaching of Scripture into practice in these real situations as they occur?

Youth Problems

1. You borrowed your Dad's car for the afternoon and bumped a concrete pillar in the car park, denting the wing.

2. You missed your period and are worried that you might be pregnant but your Mum does not know that you and your boyfriend have gone too far.

3. You do not want to continue at school to the sixth form, but want to get a job instead. Your parents still think that you want to be a teacher.

Parental Problems

1. You have just been laid off at work and the family holiday will have to be cancelled.

2. Your Mum has died, and you have to break the news to your son or daughter that their Grandma has died.

3. Your son or daughter has not been doing his or her tasks around the house and the latest school report shows a marked decline.

Pick of the pops

Aim

To encourage the young people to listen to Christian bands and artists and to help them learn to live out their Christian faith in the workplace.

Equipment

Good stereo, a selection of Christian music.
Chairs, table, etc. Paper, pencils, large sheet of paper, 2 marker pens (red and blue).

Preparation

1. Lay out the room. The panel will sit at the front. (You could go to town by bringing in a sofa, plants, standard lamp, coffee table, telephone, etc., and make this look really effective.) Have the rest of the group as the audience.

2. Write a list of songs and artists on the sheet of paper.

3. Book a Christian musician to speak (optional).

Action

1. Choose three volunteers to be music critics. (If you choose them the week before, they can come along dressed for the part.) Ask them out to the front.

2. The panel are to make comments on each of the songs and decide if it is to be a "hit" or a "miss".

3. The audience are to give each song a mark out of 100 and write it on their paper.

4. Play through 5 or 6 songs of a variety of types, including Christians who are well known; e.g. M.C. Hammer, Donna Summer, Cliff Richard, U2 as well as other Christian artists, e.g. Fat & Frantic, Amy Grant, Stryper, Petra . . . (Look in your local Christian bookshop.)

5. Thank the panel and ask the audience to hand in their marks for the different groups. Put these on one side for the moment.

6. At this point, you could bring in a local Christian musician to talk about his work and his faith and also to answer any questions. Or, divide the group into smaller groups and ask them to list the problems and difficulties facing Christian musicians in the rock business.

7. While this is happening, count up the scores for each of the artists.

8. If you have split into groups, ask each group to report back on the problems and difficulties. Ask the groups whether they think Christians should get involved in the rock business.

Talk-to

Discuss being salt and light, or what it means to be in the world but not of the world. Then let the group know which was the winning song and finish by playing it through.

Kingdom broadcast

Aim

To teach about the nature of the Kingdom and Jesus' mission.

Preparation

Copies of the Bible verses and questions for each group.

Action

Divide into four groups, and give each group a set of Bible verses, questions and a "What to do" card.

What to do

1. Read the Bible verses and discuss the questions. When you think the group has a good understanding, move on to the next part.

2. You are the Kingdom of God Party. Your task is to produce a short broadcast of three to five minutes, outlining your manifesto (i.e., what will happen if the Kingdom were to be here now, and the costs and benefits of joining your party.

3. Give the groups about 40 minutes for the task, although they may need a little more. Then get the groups to present their broadcasts to the other groups.

4. Sum up and round off.

Bible verses
Luke 4:14–21
Luke 5:21–26
Luke 6:27–31
Luke 12:29–34
Luke 13:18–20
Luke 14:15–24

Questions
1. What is the Kingdom of God?

2. How is the Kingdom of God spread?

3. Who is the Kingdom for?

4. How do you get in?

5. What does it cost to join?

6. What is it worth?

7. What are signs of the Kingdom?

Under construction

Aim

To look at the cultural gap between the Church and young people and to find ways of crossing it.

Warm-up

Play some appropriate Ice Breakers.

Equipment

Newspapers, sticky tape, cotton reels, cocktail sticks, a set of kitchen weights.

Preparation

Draw up Instruction Cards (see below).

Main session

1. Divide the group into two equal teams of between three to five young people.

2. Each team is given a cotton reel, sticky tape, a pile of newspapers, some cocktail sticks and an Instruction Card.

3. The teams have 10 minutes to plan and 20 minutes to build a bridge.

4. When they have finished, the leader measures the length of the bridge and applies the weights until the bridge breaks. Points are calculated and the winning team is announced.

Talk-to

1. Today we are looking at bridge building between the world of young people and that of the Church. What are the characteristics of both?

2. Brainstorm the characteristics on to two long pieces of paper, then put them on the wall several metres apart.

3. Give everyone a small piece of paper and ask them to write ways of bridging the gap. Use these to build a "bridge of suggestions" on the wall.

4. Ask the young people to choose the two (or more) best ideas. Taking one idea per team, plan how they would put it into action.

5. Put it into action and see what happens.

Taking your temperature

Aim

To assess where your group stands on a variety of moral, personal and spiritual issues.

Preparation

Cut out squares of coloured card – each person needs one each of nine colours. Write Bible references on other cards.

Equipment

Bibles, pencils, cards cut and sorted into colours as above, Blu-tack, four pieces of paper marked: "hot", "cold", "pro", and "anti".

Warm-up

Play a number of warm-up Ice Breakers.

Main session

1. Give each person nine cards (one of each colour) and ask them to put their name in large letters on one side and a piece of Blu-tack on the other.

2. Label one end of the room "hot" and the other end "cold", one side of the room "pro" and the other side "anti".

3. Explain to the group as follows:

a. We're going to name a number of issues, each of which has been allocated a colour.

b. For each of the issues take your card of the same colour and place it on the floor near the label which most closely identifies your feelings on the issue.

c. If you feel very concerned or an issue is important to you, place your card nearer the "hot" end of the room. If you are less concerned, place your card nearer the other end.

d. If an issue is something you feel is "right" or is one you strongly agree with, place your card on the side of the room marked "pro". But if the issue is something you feel is "wrong" or is one you disagree with, place your card on the "anti" side of the room.

e. It is possible to be very "pro" on an issue at the same time as being very "hot". Similarly, you may wish to place your card on the "anti" and "cold" section of the room.

4. Taking one issue at a time, ask each person to stick their corresponding coloured card, names uppermost, on to the floor in the part of the room which they feel represents their views.

5. When all the cards have been placed in position, let everyone have a look to see where everyone else is positioned.

Cards:

Abortion	White	Jesus	Orange
Pre-marital sex	Red	Youth group	Dark blue
Church	Yellow	Environment	Light green
School	Pale blue	Smoking	Dark green
Parents	Pink		

6. Lead into a discussion. Here are some suggestions.

a. What was the issue everyone felt most agitated about?

b. What was the issue people felt least agitated about?

c. What were people most pro and most anti on?

d. What is the group most divided about?

e. What is the group most united about?

f. How did the Church rate when compared with Jesus? Why do you think this is?

Going further

Divide into four groups and give each group a card listing a subject and Bible references (see below) to investigate and then to report back. You could deal with any number of issues.

1. *Abortion*
Jeremiah 1:5
Luke 1:39–45

2. *Pre-marital sex*
Genesis 2:24
1 Corinthians 6:12–20

3. *Parents*
Exodus 20:12
Ephesians 6:1–4

Overcomplicating Christianity

Aim

To investigate what the Christian Gospel is.

Equipment

Paper, pencils, postage stamp sized pieces of paper, Bibles, questionnaires.

Preparation

Photocopy the GNIKOOL questionnaire.

Warm-up

Hand out to everyone a copy of the GNIKOOL Questionnaire. Give them ten minutes to complete it. Share answers. (N.B. Each box on the sheet represents a word or sentence in a coded form, e.g. for number 20 the answer is "Looking backwards".)

Talk-to

Some people think that Christianity is like the quiz: rather complex and full of tricks. Today we are looking at what Christianity really is . . .

Main session

1. Ask the group to write on the stamp sized pieces of paper what the Christian Gospel really is . . . Allow them about five

1	2	3	4
N W O T	SAND	PROGRAMME	PUT KILOGRAM

5	6	7	8
CHEEKKEEHC	ANOTHER ANOTHER ANOTHER ANOTHER ANOTHER ANOTHER	KNEE ――― LIGHTS	MAN ――― BOARD

9	10	11	12
W I N D	――― BSc PhD MSc	R O ROADS D S	OHONLEE

13	14	15	16
GROUND FEET FEET FEET FEET FEET FEET	CHAIR	ON LAP LAP LAP	N I P

17	18	19	20
T R A WORLD L E V	BELT ――― HITTING	J U YOU AND ME S T	GNIKOOL

Answers

1 .... 2 .... 3 .... 4 ....

5 .... 6 .... 7 .... 8 ....

9 .... 10 .... 11 .... 12 ....

13 .... 14 .... 15 .... 16 ....

17 .... 18 .... 19 .... 20 ....

minutes to do this, then gather back and let them share what they wrote.

2. Pass out the Bibles and list the following verses where everyone can see them:

John 1:12   Acts 4:12
John 3:16–18   Romans 3:23–24
Acts 13:38

3. In pairs, the group should look up the verses. Then using the Bible verses and their first stamp sized Gospels, write a joint "What is the Christian Gospel" in few enough words to fit on a stamp.

4. When all the pairs have done this, ask them again to share their Gospels with the group.

Talk-to

It is possible to have all sorts of strange ideas of what Christianity is all about, but the Bible tells us which of these is right and wrong. If we imagine our Christian life as a journey, then the Bible is our map and guide book and the Holy Spirit is our guide. Close with prayer.

Quiz answers

1. Up town
2. Sand box
3. Space programme
4. Put on weight
5. Cheek to cheek
6. Six of one and half a dozen of the other
7. Neon lights
8. Man over board
9. Down wind
10. 3 degrees under.
11. Crossroads
12. Hole in one
13. Six feet under ground
14. High chair
15. On the last lap
16. Pin up
17. Travel around the world
18. Hitting below the belt
19. Just between you and me
20. Looking backwards

Ice cream evangelism

Aim

To look at the opportunities and the problems of personal evangelism. The activity can also be used as a discussion starter on the uniqueness of Christ.

Preparation

Write one-minute topic cards.

Equipment

Bibles, paper, pens, dice, a large sheet of paper, one-minute topic cards and a marker pen.

Warm-up

1.   Everyone sits in a circle.

2.   Each person rolls the dice in turn. If a six is thrown, that person must take a one-minute topic card and talk on that topic for one minute. If a number between 1 and 5 is thrown, the dice is simply passed on to the next person.

3.   Keep the one-minute topic cards face down so that nobody knows what they say before they are chosen.

Topic cards

1. My pet elephant	6. Warfare
2. School dinners	7. Vegetarians
3. Sunday lunch	8. My best day
4. Jesus	9. Blue
5. Church	10. Radio

Main session

1. Ask each person to decide what their favourite ice cream flavour is and then to get into groups with people of the same taste in ice cream. Ask the groups to say what their flavour is and the number in their group. Record this on a large displayed sheet of paper.

2. Explain now that their task is to persuade everyone else that their group's flavour is the best to be had in ice cream and try to get them to join their group. Give them three minutes for this.

3. Now ask everyone to regather into their new groups and find the new numbers in each group. Put the figures on to the large sheet of paper. There is likely to be very little change.

4. Tell the groups that they have two minutes in which to plan a strategy by which folk from other groups might be persuaded to join their particular group. Give them two minutes.

5. Meanwhile, pick out one member from the whole group (pick two people if the group is greater than 14). Take him or her aside and explain that they have just discovered that ice cream is a slow and deadly poison leading to inevitable death. Their task is to persuade people not to eat it. Introduce this person and give him or her a further three minutes to try and persuade people not to eat ice cream.

6. When the time is up, write down the final figures on the record sheet.

De-brief

How many people changed sides?
Why did people swap?
Why did people stay?
How many people responded to the poison warning?
Why did some people not respond?
Are there any similarities between Christianity and ice cream evangelism?

You may want to draw out these parallels:
1. All religions lead to death; Jesus is the only way to the Father (John 14:16).

2. Not many people are persuaded by argument to swap sides. Is this true when talking to people about Christianity?

3. If people were forced into other groups, did they return to their original groups soon afterwards? Is this like non-Christians who are made to attend church?

Going further

Divide the group into small groups of four and give them paper and pencils. Ask each group to look at evangelism in the New Testament using the verses given below. From this information, can they think of any ways to reach out to their friends, family and neighbours? Then ask all the groups to report back.

Helpful verses
1. 1 Corinthians 2:1–5
2. Acts 4:32–35
3. Matthew 28:19–20
4. John 14:15–17
5. Matthew 5:13–16

The body of Christ

Aim

To investigate what Scripture means by the term "The Body of Christ".

Warm-up

Use some good "body games" e.g. Body connections or Mirrors (in *Youthbuilders*).

Equipment

Paper, pencils, Bibles, paint, card, Blu-tack.

Preparation

Cut out a large body shape from paper or from a roll of wallpaper.

Talk-to

Explain that the Church is often described in Scripture as the "Body of Christ". Today we will be trying to learn more about what that means. Read 1 Corinthians 12:12–20.

Action

1.   Brainstorm all the parts of the body (internal and external), writing them on a large sheet of paper. (Inevitably someone will suggest the sexual organs and it is up to you to decide whether to include them. When we did this activity, I put them on the flipchart, but not in the slang form in which they were suggested.) Then ask them to think of the youth group as a body, and decide which bit of the body they think they are and why (and not to tell anyone).

2.   Pass out paper, card, pens, scissors, paint, crayons, etc. and ask everyone to make the part of the body which is most like them.

3.   When everyone has finished, sit in a semi-circle facing the large paper person on the wall and ask them to explain which bit of the body they are and attach themselves to the paper person in the appropriate place on the body. Examples "I'm a liver because I'm always cleaning up the mess at the end of the evening." "I'm an arm, because I always move the equipment." "I'm an eye because I notice if anyone is upset."

4.   Either in discussion or in groups, ask these questions:
What parts of the body are missing on the paper body?
What are their functions?
What might their functions be in this group?

What effect does their absence have on the group's functioning.

5.   The groups then report back.

Going further

Some people think that spiritual gifts are similar to natural talents, so let's see how many spiritual gifts we know. Here are some Bible verses to help.

Romans 12:1–8
1 Corinthians 12:1–11
Ephesians 4:11–13

Action

1.   Brainstorm spiritual gifts on to paper or flipchart.

2.   Go down the list asking who in the group has or does not have any of these gifts.

Talk-to

1.   Everybody who is a Christian has the Holy Spirit (Ephesians 1:13).

2.   God gives gifts to different people at different times, e.g., one day he may use you to bring a word of knowledge or anoint you with power for healing; the next day he will anoint someone else.

3.   Just because God has used us does not make us different from or more important than our brothers and sisters in Christ.

4.   We must decide to be used by God: He will not use us if we are not open to Him.

5.   We can distinguish between gifts and ministries – if we find God giving us the same gift on a regular basis over time, it may be that this is a "ministry".

6.   Answer any questions and close with appropriate prayer.

Fruit of the Spirit

Aim

To learn about the fruit of the Spirit.

Equipment

Fruit juice cocktail containing as wide a variety of jucies as you can find. Paper, pencils, fruit score cards, Bibles, paper cups.

Preparation

Mix the fruit cocktail; photocopy fruit score cards.

Warm-up

Play some energetic games from *Youthbuilders*, or from Ice Breakers section.

Main session

1. Give everyone a cup of the fruit cocktail and ask them to write on their pieces of paper the ingredients they can taste.

2. Read out the ingredients and find out how many recognised each one. Were there any ingredients they could taste that were not in the cocktail?

3. *Talk to*: The fruit of the Spirit can be compared to the fruit cocktail. There is one fruit but it has many flavours. Who knows what they are? List these on a flipchart, OHP or paper.

If the group do not know, help them out with the last few. Then read Galatians 5:16–26.

4. Hand out a fruit score card to each person.

5. For each of the characteristics, ask members to give themselves a score out of 10 and then give the group a score.

6. In groups of three or four, share these answers and encourage comment on how people see themselves and how they see the group.

Discussion

1. Were there any areas where the group scored very low? Why do you think this is?

2. Were there any areas where people as individuals scored very low? Why did you think this is?

3. Did any individuals have a personal score that the members of the small group disagreed with?

Talk-to

"The fruit of the Spirit is not like the gifts of the Spirit. With the gifts, we as Christians may have one but perhaps not another. But all the different flavours of fruit should be showing through in our daily lives. The fruit of the Spirit is the product of the Holy Spirit working in our lives, and so if we are not producing fruit then maybe we are not letting the Holy Spirit work in certain areas. If you put a black sheet on an area of your lawn at home, the grass will grow yellow and die. Similarly, if areas of our lives are cut off from the Spirit we need to repent of our sins and offer ourselves to the Holy Spirit. Then the fruit will grow."

Close with a time of confession and a time of asking the Holy Spirit to fill everyone to overflowing.

Fruit score card		
	ME	*GROUP*
Love		
Joy		
Kindness		
Patience		
Self-control		
Peace		
Goodness		
Gentleness		
Faithfulness		

GROUP BUILDERS

Group Builders are opportunities for the group to grow – not in numbers but in quality of relationship.

Group Builders develop the youth group's identity and the members' sense of belonging. They give opportunities for members' leadership potential to develop whilst helping the young people to be honest with each other about their strengths and weaknesses.

It is important to be sensitive to the situations and needs of individuals when debriefing these exercises. Strong emotions are best expressed. Give plenty of opportunity for people to say how they feel or felt.

Pictures of me

Aim

To encourage the youth group to share honestly about themselves and to build up the group.

Equipment

Paint, pens, glue, tissue, magazines, glitter, leaves, foil, large sheets of paper.

Preparation

Duplicate "Who am I?" questionnaires.

Warm-up

Pass out "Who am I?" questionnaires. When everyone has finished, share the answers, either in small groups or together.

Action

1. Tell them they have half an hour to produce a picture of themselves using the materials provided. This picture could represent anything which is like them. History, emotions, character, likes/dislikes, strengths/weaknesses, physical appearance, hopes, fears, etc.

2. When the time is up, gather round and each person talks about the picture he or she made.

3. Close by passing round a Bible and while each one holds it the rest of the group pray for that person.

Questionnaire: Who am I?

Name

Nickname

Age
Favourite number
Favourite colour
What size are your feet?
What is your favourite food?
How many cousins do you have?
What is your favourite pop group?
What is your most embarrassing moment?

What is your ambition in life?

What is your biggest fear?

What is your funniest experience?

Who would you most like to meet?
What are your interests and hobbies?

What is the most important thing in your life?

What is your favourite sport?
Who is your favourite TV personality?
Do you go to church?
If yes, how often?
What was your favourite youth group meeting?

What is one thing you would like to get out of this weekend/
evening?

What is one thing you feel could contribute to this weekend/
evening?

Hagglenosh

Aim

To encourage working together and sharing.

Equipment

Food and equipment to feed all your group (see Preparation section), allowing 2 sausages and 2 slices of bread per person.

Preparation

Copy the instruction sheets.
   Put the food and equipment in rooms as follows:

Kitchen	Room 1	Room 2	Room 3
cooker	sausages	plates	butter
ice cream	bread	bowls	knives
kettle	milk	tea	saucepan
baked beans	frying pan	spoons	forks
		coffee	mugs

Action

1.   Divide the group into four teams with a minimum of three in each team. (If you have less than 12 members, see variations at the end). The red team goes in the kitchen, blue in Room 1, Green in Room 2, Yellow in Room 3.

2.   Hand out the instruction sheet.

Hints

1. Use your leaders as observers, explaining the rules, reminding people of the time and ensuring that there is no cheating.

2. The results are very variable. Some youth groups will end up all eating together, others will never come to a solution. In some youth groups only some of the teams will eat. It all helps to teach about sharing.

Variations

If you have fewer than 12 members, divide as follows:

Kitchen	Room 1	Room 2
cooker	sausages	frying pan
ice cream	milk	saucepan
kettle		mugs

Distribute the rest of the food and equipment by writing their names on cards and randomly distributing.

Instructions

1. Each team's task is to have supper.
2. Each team comprises the following people:

a) Foreign Secretary: You may negotiate with another team or teams but only at the U.N. (a circle of chairs set up in a neutral position and labelled U.N.). You may not enter any foreign countries; you may only negotiate your team's agreed position.

b) Ambassador: You can enter foreign countries if they let you, either to give a message or to receive a message to bring back. You may not negotiate.

c) 1 or 2 Reporters: You can observe what is happening in another country but are not allowed to talk outside your own country.

3. When visiting another group, a person must inform them of his or her status, but a group does not have to let anyone into their territory.

4. Summit meetings at the U.N. can be attended by Reporters and Ambassadors as observers, but only the Foreign Secretary is allowed to be taken to the U.N.

5. Only the red team are allowed to do the cooking.

6. You have one hour to complete the task.

You're the leader

Aim

To encourage the youth group towards a Christian perspective on pastoral situations within the group.

Equipment

Paper, pens, Bibles.

Preparation

Write out Pastoral Problem cards.

Action

1. Divide into groups of three or four.

2. Give each group a Pastoral Problem card. They then have 20 minutes to decide what they would do if they were the group leader.

3. Each group in turn reports back, explaining what the issues were in each situation and how they would handle them.

4. When all the groups have reported back, ask them to put themselves in the position of the person needing help and ask how they would feel if they were cared for in each of the ways proposed.

5. Close with prayer.

Problem 1

You are woken up in the early hours of the morning by a continual ringing on the doorbell.

On answering the door, you find Jane, desperately upset, sobbing and apologising for waking you.

When you sit her down with a drink she begins to explain that the relationship between her and Mike (also in the youth group) has "gone too far".

You discover that they have had sexual intercourse on a few occasions, knowing it to be wrong, and have been trying desperately hard to stop. They have just had another row after failing to control their sexual urges once again.

Jane is feeling guilty, away from God, dirty, cheap and frightened of becoming pregnant, and also of her parents finding out.

How will you help and advise Jane?
Should you speak to Mike?

Problem 2

Ron grew up in a strict Christian environment. Although his parents were good people, they seemed to be very protective towards him when it came to his social life.

Ron was not allowed to go out to the cinema or to discos with his friends because – in the eyes of his parents – his friends were not good enough for him.

He was not rebellious, but his parents' strict attitude caused a lot of tension. All his parents wanted him to do was go to church or youth group. Ron wanted to do other things, too.

At 16, Ron began to lie to his parents about where he was going. He said he was going to the youth group, but was actually going out with friends for milkshakes, etc. Ron was doing nothing wrong or illegal with his friends. He was beginning to feel a bit guilty about deceiving his parents, but he could not bring himself to tell them what he was doing.

How would you help Ron?
If Ron's Mum phoned and asked whether he was at youth group, what would you tell her?

Problem 3

Emma was one of the best dancers at school. She had won a couple of disco dance awards and was always full of energy. Both her parents worked hard and expected Emma to do well at school. They also expected her to look "just right' – they always allowed her money to buy the latest fashions. Her father, whom she adored, occasionally teased Emma about acquiring some "love handles" around her mid-section.

Emma confided her concern about her weight to a close friend, who told Emma about a new diet she was on. She explained in detail how she always took laxatives and induced vomiting after eating. The claim was that the nutrients got into the body, but the calories were flushed down the toilet.

Emma tried the diet and it worked for a while. But she soon became obsessed with food. She would sometimes eat meals large enough for several people and then go to the bathroom and induce vomiting. After a while, her parents and friends noticed a change in Emma's personality. She seemed to be continually tired and her behaviour was a little strange.

Emma's condition is drawn to your attention. How will you help her?

Problem 4

Helen is an outgoing, friendly and committed member of the youth group. One evening she comes to the group with a black eye, telling her friends that she slipped on the kitchen floor and banged her head against the work surface.

During a quiet moment you approach her, making a joke about her black eye. She immediately bursts into tears and explains between sobs that her father, a regular attender at the church, has an alcohol problem. He is often drunk when Helen gets home from school so she generally avoids him by going straight to her room.

On this occasion, her Mum and Dad were arguing and Helen tried to prevent her Dad from striking her Mum. In the ensuing conflict, Helen was struck by her father.

What action or advice would you offer in these circumstances?

Problem 5

Dave comes to the youth group regularly with a group of friends. While on a youth weekend, you visit the town together and realise that Dave has disappeared. He is later discovered in the arcade playing the games machines. He's bragging about getting the highest score on "Star Wars" but then tells you reluctantly that he has spent over £15 on the machines.

Dave comes from a wealthy family where he has his own computer games, but his parents will not give him enough money to feed his growing addiction to the arcade machines; he goes there every day after school.

He also admits that he's beginning to steal things from shops and sell them to his friends to finance his habit.

Dave's school grades have dropped and he's become more isolated from his friends. He realises he has a problem and wants help.

How will you help him?

Honest truth

Aim

To enable the group to be honest about each other when describing each other's good and bad points and to increase group awareness.

Number

Any number.

Equipment

A set of cards as listed below but alter them to fit the particular needs of your group. Use sheets of A4 paper cut into 8 pieces.

Preparation

Write out the cards.

Action

1. Everyone is seated in a circle and the cards are placed face down in the middle.

2. Choose a person (A) to draw the first card. That person reads it silently and then gives it to the person it best describes (B).

3. (B) can choose whether or not to read out the card he or she has been given to the rest of the group.

4.   (B) then takes a card from the middle and reads it silently. (B) then passes it to the person it best describes.

5.   This continues until all the cards have been used. Some people will have lots of cards, some will have a few and some perhaps none at all.

De-brief

1.   All the group reads their cards in turn, prefixing each statement with "I am . . ." if they agree, or "Someone thinks that I am . . ." if they disagree.

2.   At the end, each person has the opportunity to give one of their own cards to someone in the group who they feel it more accurately describes.

3.   Each person can also then take one card from someone else if they wish, to add it to their own set of cards.

4.   Ask the group at this stage: Who is happy with their cards and who is not?

5.   Each person in turn may take another card from anyone's pile and give it to someone else.

6.   When the group have completed this, ask again: Who is happy with their cards and who is not?

7.   Everyone then reads their cards again, saying "I am . . ." or "The group feels that I am . . ."

8.   Talk to the group, ensuring that they feel affirmed and "built up" rather than "knocked down". Assure them of their acceptance by God and end with prayer.

Hints

This exercise can produce a strong emotional response. This may initially be on a superficial level, but as the task progresses do not be surprised if there is a marked change in your young people as they begin to realize how other people see them. Sometimes there are tears, as other times there is lots of laughter, but there is always increased openness and a growing together. Be prepared, though, to talk, pray and spend time with people afterwards. Also, ensure that your behaviour towards the group always reinforces God's acceptance of them.

Cards
The easiest person to talk to . . .

The girl who talks to the boys the most . . .

The person who thinks the most about others . . .

The person who is the most generous . . .

The most dominant person . . .

The person who makes me feel the most frustrated . . .

The most sensitive person . . .

The most forgiving person . . .

The person furthest from Christ . . .

The most honest person . . .

The person with the nicest eyes . . .

The person with the nicest hair . . .

The person with the most kissable lips . . .

(Add about 25 more.)

Lego towers

Aim

A team work exercise.

Preparation

Photocopy points scoring sheets and instructions.

Equipment

Bags of 350 lego bricks (size 4×2), points scoring sheets and instructions.

How to play

1. Divide the group into teams of four and position the teams out of sight of each other.

2. Give each team a copy of the instructions and a point scoring sheet. Then let them play!

3. After the towers are built, measure them, count up the bricks and the time and calculate the winner.

4. Discuss together:
    Who was the leader?
    How did the group work together?
    Was everyone included?
    What hindered the task?
    Why did some teams do better than others?

Talk-to

Talk about what the task of Christianity is and how we can achieve it, or about the Body of Christ and working together.

Instructions

1. You are to build a tower which scores maximum points (see graphs).

2. The tower must be self-supporting.

3. You have 25 minutes to plan the tower and a maximum of 10 minutes to build it.

4. During the planning stage, you may assemble bricks but these must be detached before the building phase.

5. On completion the points scored will be calculated and the team scoring the most is the winner.

Points score sheet (refer to graphs)
Height (cm): .... Score ....
No. of bricks: .... Score ....
Time (mins): .... Score ....
Total score ....

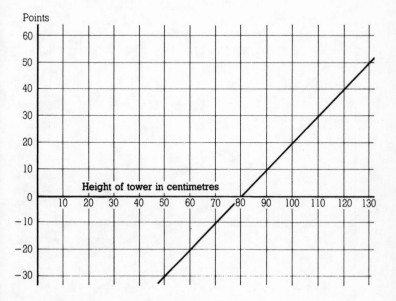

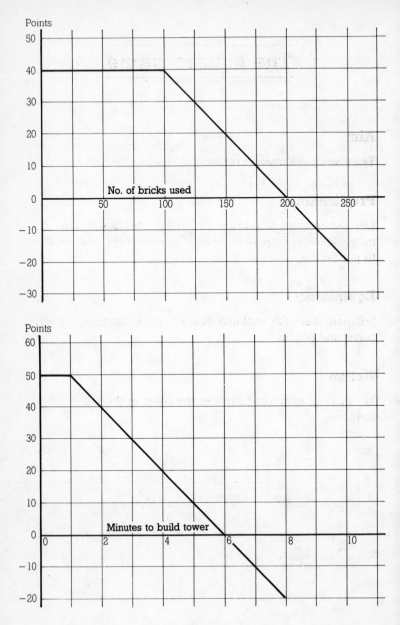

The square game

Aim

Team work discussion exercise.

Preparation

Lay out a court measuring 3m by 3m, containing nine one-metre squares. Prepare numbered cards and the solution sheet to put on the wall.

Equipment

Solution sheet (as outlined below), cards numbered 1 to 8, paper and pencils

Action

1.   Lay out numbered cards in the court in the following pattern.

7	1	3
2		5
6	4	8

Put the solution sheet on the wall.

1	2	3
4	5	6
7	8	

2. Brief the group as follows. Eight players are needed. Each of them should stand in one of the squares containing a numbered card. The task is for the group to rearrange the players to conform with the solution sheet, but the following rules must be noted.

3. Rules:
    No talking.
    Players can step forwards, backwards, or sideways.
    No one can move diagonally.
    Players can move only into an empty space.
    Only one player can be in any one square at a time.
    Cards may not be exchanged.
    Players may not move out of the grid.
    Those who are not playing should be given paper and pencils to observe the group.

4. On the order to start, the group should begin to work towards the solution. Allow them about 20 minutes in silence, and then if they show little sign of completing the task, allow them to talk.

5. After 40 minutes, or when the task has been completed, gather everyone around to debrief and discuss the activity.

De-brief

1. Who moved first and how did they decide to move?

2. How were moves organized?

3. Did people use non-verbal communication? How?

4. Did people make verbal communication?

5. Was everyone aware of everyone else's number?

6. Who felt frustrated, annoyed, etc.? Why?

7. Who facilitated and who blocked the task?

Going further

What is the task of a Christian youth group? What facilitates or blocks that task?

Lost on the moon!

Aim

Team work, decision making and consensus seeking.

Equipment

Photocopied "Lost on the moon" sheets and copies of the NASA Rankings, pencils.

How to play

1.   Divide the group into smaller units of between five and seven members.

2.   Each person is given a copy of the "Lost on the moon" sheet. The task is to rank each item in order of importance for the group's survival. (It is important that, initially, this is done individually.)

118

3.   After everyone has completed the list, it is now the task of the small group to come to a corporate list upon which they all agree.

4.   When the group list is done, pass out the NASA result sheets and ask everyone to score how well they did, firstly as individuals and then as a group unit.

5.   The group finds its error marks by calculating the difference between their ranking on any particular item and NASA's. To survive, a person's error ratio must be less than 20.

6.   Discussion together:
     Which individuals survived and which did not?
     Which teams survived?
     Were the group surprised at any of the rankings?
     Which ones and why?
     How did each group decide where their priorities began?
     Was this different from the way in which individuals decided the same thing?
     What was done in the groups with those members who disagreed?
     Who was the leader? etc.

Lost on the moon!
Your spaceship has just crashed on the moon. You are sched-
uled to rendezvous with a mother ship 200 miles away on the
lighted surface of the moon, but the rough landing has ruined
your ship and destroyed all the equipment on board except for
the 15 items listed below. Your crew's survival depends on
reaching the mother ship, so you must choose the most critical
items available for the 200 mile trip. Your task is to rank the
items in order of their importance for survival. Place number
1 by the most important item through to number 15 for the
least important.

.... Box of matches
.... Food concentrate
.... Fifty feet of nylon rope
.... Parachute silk
.... Solar-powered portable heating unit
.... Two .45 calibre pistols
.... One case of dehydrated milk
.... Two 100-pound tanks of oxygen
.... Stellar map of the moon's constellation
.... Self-inflating life raft
.... Magnetic compass
.... Five gallons of water
.... Signal flares
.... First Aid kit containing injection needles
.... Solar-powered FM-receiver-transmitter

Lost on the Moon: Solution

Items	NASA's reasoning	NASA's ranks	Your ranks	Error points
Box of matches	No oxygen on moon to sustain flame; virtually worthless	15		
Food concentrate	Efficient means of supplying energy requirements	4		
Fifty feet of nylon rope	Useful in scaling cliffs, tying injured together	6		
Parachute silk	Protection from sun's rays	8		
Solar-powered portable heating unit	Not needed unless on the dark side	13		
Two .45 calibre pistols	Possible means of self-propulsion	11		
One case of dehydrated milk	Bulkier duplication of food concentrate	12		
Two 100-pound tanks of oxygen	Most pressing survival need	1		
Stellar map	Primary means of navigation	3		
Self-inflating life raft	CO_2 bottle in military raft may be used for propulsion	9		
Magnetic compass	Magnetic field on moon is not polarised; worthless for navigation	14		
Five gallons of water	Replacement for tremendous liquid loss on lighted side	2		
Signal flares	Distress signal when mother ship is sight	10		
First Aid kit	Needles for victims, medicine, etc., will fit special aperture in NASA space suits	7		
Solar-powered FM receiver-trans.	For communication with mother ship; but FM requires line-of-sight transmission and short ranges	5		

121

DOWN THE POLE!

These activities help young people to put their Christianity into action.

It is often said, "What we hear we forget, but what we do we remember," Jesus sent out his disciples to do what they had seen him doing. I'm sure that after they came back from healing the sick and proclaiming the Kingdom, they would have watched Jesus twice as carefully so that they could see how they should do things better the next time He sent them off on a faith-sharing visit.

Unfortunately, too much of our Christianity is made up of passive listening or mentally assenting to the right doctrines, rather than the active faith demonstrated by Jesus.

Young People like causing a stir and being challenged. When we built a Shanty House in the middle of Haslemere High Street and sat drinking tea from empty baked bean tins, the young people loved talking about what they were doing, why they were doing it and what church they were from. They were surprised by those supposedly Christian people who hurried by, too embarrassed to stop. It gave the story of the Good Samaritan a whole new slant!

This Down the Pole! section gives "doing" ideas for Christian young people who want to demonstrate the Kingdom of God in action.

Prayer for the world

Aim

To encourage the youth group prayer life, to raise awareness of issues and to have fun, by holding an all-night prayer vigil.

Equipment

Pens, paper, candles, OHP, musicians, information on the issues you want to cover, coffee, hot chocolate, biscuits.

Preparation

Choose an issue for a night of prayer and activities, e.g. Evangelism, Abortion, World Peace, Unemployment, Homelessness, etc. Gather information from Christian organisations working in the area. Book your church for the night and make arrangements for the heating to be on. Hire any videos, cassettes, etc. Write letters to youth group parents explaining what you are planning to do. If you are a very small youth group, write and invite others to join you.

Action

The night will need to be planned out in half-hour sessions with a mixture of movement, stillness, activity, quiet, noise, etc. Include the following ingredients:

1.   Praise and worship: Acknowledging God for who He is and what He has done for us.

2.   Adoration: Quiet songs expressing our love for God.

3. Meditation: Taize chants, Scripture and psalms sung reflectively.

4. Prayers:
    Individual – intercessions, quiet or out loud.
    Pairs – for specifics and each other.
    Groups – open intercession on the issues.

5. Movement: Pray in different parts of the building for different aspects of the issue. A prayer night for abortion victims, for example, could go like this:

By the pulpit:	Pray that we would speak God's Word out and be His prophets in the world.
By the cross:	Pray for us to have the same love for sinners as Christ had for us.
By the baptistry:	Pray for forgiveness when we have failed to speak out and act.
By the Lord's Table:	Pray that we may learn to become Christ in the world, offering healing.
In a corner:	Pray for victims suffering alone.
By the door:	Pray for those entering the church who suffer because of past sin and hurt in this area.

6. Light and dark: Use candles, symbolizing light and dark, Christ the light of the world; or meditate on a Scripture verse with a single candle as the only light.

7. Action: Provide resources so that the Youth Group can be informed on the issue.
    a) Watch a video, listen to a tape, read articles and link these with something to do – a collage, posters, drama, dance, a song.
    b) Give the group some Bible passages to study and report back on.
    c) Construct a Scripture banner appropriate to the issue to hang in church.

8.   Refreshments: Serve drinks and nibbles at regular intervals through the night and make sure there is access to a toilet. Set aside space for people to crash out. (Make it somewhere visible, or have separate male and female areas.) In the morning, have breakfast together before going home or to church for the morning service.

9.   Publicity: Take a black and white photo and write a press release for your local paper on what you have done.

Suggested programme for an all-night vigil

8.00 pm	Arrive and sign in
8.10 pm	Worship and praise
8.30 pm	Video and discussion
9.15 pm	Pairs and group prayers on topics from discussing
10.00 pm	Coffee break
10.15 pm	Bible study in groups of four
11.00 pm	Sharing of study results
11.15 pm	Moving prayer
12.00 pm	Coffee break
12.30 am	Activity 1: Drama, dance or collages on the issue
1.15 am	Tape by a Christian artist
1.25 am	Teaching tape
1.45 am	Prayer in pairs
2.00 am	Coffee break
2.15 am	What can we do? Bible verses and action plan
3.00 am	Quiet
3.15 am	Taize Song: quiet song by a single candle
3.20 am	Pass lights out to every person, pray for individual responsibility to be lights in the world. Then light all candles.
3.35 am	Open prayer
4.00 am	Coffee break
4.15 am	Activity 2: Banner for church, article for newsletter, letter writing to papers or MP, etc.
6.00 am	Coffee break
6.15 am	Worship and praise
7.00 am	Breakfast!

Parents' meal

Aim

1. To get all the youth group together, both church and "non-churched", and to provide an opportunity for evangelism.

2. To enable the youth group to work together on a project and learn about their strengths, weaknesses, gifts, etc.

Numbers

As many of the youth group as possible, plus their parents.

Preparation

1. Get the youth group together and describe the idea to them.

2. Brainstorm all that needs to be done, e.g. menus planned, room decorated, tickets made, food bought and prepared . . . (Let them do the thinking.)

3. Organize a leader for each of the tasks, e.g.
    a. Chief chef: to organize buying and cooking of food.
    b. Head waiter/waitress: to organize serving staff, layout of the room and table decoration.
    c. Entertainments manager: to organize the entertainment, any evangelistic talks, sketches, etc.
    d. Publicity officer: to design invitations and tickets.
    e. Treasurer: to handle the money.
    If you have a small group, everyone will have a job. But even with a larger group of young people (14 to 18), every-

one will be needed as waiting staff, as cooks or for the entertainment.

Action

Once you have outlined the idea, motivated your young people and formed your committee, you need to decide on the menu. Our group decided on two choices of starter, main course and dessert, but encouraged parents to make their choice when they purchased their tickets, so that the exact amounts needed were known well in advance. It is good to decide on a theme for your meal. It could be a formal occasion with waiting staff in "black tie" outfits, or it could have a national theme such as Mexican or French, with the appropriate decor.

Hints

The first time we did this, it was as a fundraiser for the youth group. It was only the next morning when a number of parents arrived at church for the first time that we realized the evangelistic possibilities.

Try intermingling the church and non-church parents in the seating plan. Also, unless you have skilled caterers in your group, keep it simple!

Sample menu
Soup or Prawn Cocktail
Roast Chicken or Lasagne
Potatoes and vegetables
Fresh fruit salad and cream
or Fruit crumble and custard
Coffee & Mints

Shanty house

Aim

1. To put Bible teaching on the Third World into action.

2. To raise money or gain publicity for a project.

3. To help the young people articulate their faith.

Objective

To build a Shanty House in a prominent position in town and use it as a focus for a day's activities on the theme of poverty. Imagine the situation . . .

"It was 5 am, the sun was coming up as we began dumping the rusted sheets of corrugated iron and old sack out of the car in the pedestrianized shopping area. A dozen young people set to work nailing and roping it together. Yes, believe it or not, in the midst of Cheltenham Spa, a shanty house was being built . . . Throughout the day we talked, surveyed and collected – raising money and also people's awareness."

Preparation

1. Talk the idea through with your young people and get them interested.

2. Involve them in the preparatory work. You will need permission from:
   a. The police
   b. The borough engineers
   c. The highway department if necessary.

3. Collect materials. We had a wooden frame and some pre-assembled sections on to which corrugated iron, flattened tin cans, plastic sheeting, pieces of sack, etc., could be attached.

4. Prepare questionnaires, collect publicity material.

5. If you decide to raise money for something, have information and displays.

6. Invite local press, TV and radio.

Action

1. Meet early on the day so that everything can be set up before the shops open.

2. Have a rota of young people to be at the Shanty House to answer questions.

3. Cook a simple meal on a fire, serve coffee in tin cans, etc.

Options

Combine this with a number of social concern activities, such as a fast or drama.

Hints

1. Have a clear aim for the day. This might be to conduct a survey, or to raise people's awareness on an issue such as clean water or homelessness.

2. Good information and publicity material, especially posters, can be obtained from Tear Fund. They can also give you hints on how to build your house. (Tear Fund, Education Dept., 100 Church Road, Teddington, Middx. TW11 8QE.)

3. Encourage the young people to talk about why they are concerned for others as part of their Christian faith. There may be good opportunities for personal evangelism.

Parents' shopping breaks

Aim

For the youth group to run Christmas activities for children on a Saturday morning to let parents do their Christmas shopping while their kids have a great time.

Action

1. Suggest the idea to the youth group, either as a service to the project or as a fundraiser.

2. Decide on the time and dates, eg. the last two Saturday mornings before Christmas from 9 am until 12.30 pm. Book the hall. Produce publicity posters to inform parents well in advance.

3. Distribute letters to all church parents with the right aged children, using a return slip for them to book their children for either or both of the days.

4. Get the helpers together to plan the activities and make a list of the materials needed. Possible activities include:

Christmas decoration making	Videos
Christmas card making	Games
Cooking and icing	Singing
Stories	Painting

5. On the day itself, make sure everything is set up and all the helpers are ready to start before the children arrive. When they do, find out if any of the children have special needs (e.g. not allowed orange squash) and what time they will be collected.

6.   Teenagers and children then have a great time: three hours of getting themselves and everything else covered in glitter, paint, tissue paper, glue and icing . . . plus making a few things to take home.

7.   Clear up and have a cup of tea to recover.

Hints

1.   You may find some potential recruits for Junior Church or Sunday School – both children and leaders! Teenage lads who previously thought that they didn't like kids can find that it is great fun and become helpers.

2.   Have a few different activities for the second week if the same children are to come.

Video freeze frame

Aim

To get young people out and on to the streets, talking to people about their faith, and to produce a discussion resource for the youth group, church house groups, etc.

Equipment

A video camera and TV monitor. If you have access to editing equipment as well, it can be great fun, if not the group will have to edit on camera.

Action

1.   Introduce the youth group to the camera and equipment. If you have borrowed it from your local youth office or denominational regional HQ, ask if someone will come over and demonstrate how to use it all! Let the youth group use it, get used to it and feel relaxed. (This will help you and them see who has the talents required for the task.)

2.   Choose an area of Christian concern or of particular interest to the group, e.g., Death, Jesus, Heaven and Hell, Being born again, Church, War. Then list a number of questions on the chosen subject, e.g., What happens to you when you die? Do you believe that Jesus rose from the dead?

3.   Find two or three volunteers who are willing to go out on a Saturday morning and film people answering the questions.

4.   When interviewing, the young people need to say where they are from and why they are doing it.

5.   Show the film next time the youth group meets and use it
as a discussion starter for a Bible study on the chosen topic.

Hints

We did this exercise on the issue of Death and only met one
church-goer, but it enabled questions to be asked that could
never have been asked of strangers in the street normally.

Parable of the talents

Aim

To teach a biblical parable in a memorable way and to raise funds for the youth group.

Equipment

Paper, pencils, Bibles, questions, envelopes numbered 1 to 4 containing different amounts of money: £10, £5, £2, £1.

Action

1. Divide the youth group into groups of four or five, including those who are absent, so that every member is included in a team.

2. Tell them that each group will be given an envelope containing an amount of money (for greater impact use your own money if you can afford it). They have to use it to its best advantage and make the most profit with it. Tell them that in a few weeks' time (but do not specify exactly when), you will call them to account for what they have done.

3. Each group chooses a number and receives the envelope with that number on. They can open the envelope and see how much money they have to spend. They then have to plan how they are going to use the money most profitably, write down their action plan and hand it in.

4. When all the groups have done this, tell them that no one will know when they will be called to account, then play an appropriate ice breaker.

Follow-up

1.   Six weeks later, ask the young people to get back into their teams and choose one person from each team to report back to the whole group on how they used the money and if they made any profit.

2.   When all the groups have reported, congratulate them on how they did. Give them a Bible and question sheet and ask them to answer the questions in their group.

3.   When the groups have finished and reported back, give everyone a piece of paper. Ask them to write on it any talents they would like God to use in their lives that have so far been unused. If they would like to use these talents in youth group or in Church, ask them to hand them in.

4.   Close with prayers.

5.   After the meeting is over, pray for those who have handed in talent papers and with your elder, minister or vicar see how their gifts can be used in church.

Questions
1.   Read Matthew 25:14–30.

2.   Are there any similarities between the parable and the exercise that you have done?

3.   Which of the groups was like which of the servants in the parable?

4.   When Jesus is talking about talents, is He talking about money?

5.   If not, then what is He talking about?

6.   What talents do you feel you do not use as God intended?

Youth day

Aim

Young people are not just souls to be saved but whole people with spiritual, emotional, mental, physical, and social needs. Holding a Youth Day or Weekend can meet some of those needs for the young people of your area, as well as mobilizing your own youth group and giving them a chance to demonstrate the Gospel.

Action

1. Get your youth group to discuss the possibilities – what events would work and what would not, where to hold the

event, what time of year, etc. This planning is best done in the autumn, six months before the event will take place. Activities could include:

Fun run	Stalls (Tombola, raffle, etc.)
Disco	Bouncy Castle
Dancing display	Barbeque
Gymnastics	Sports events
Black Tie Ball	Scout and Guide displays
Rock Band Competition	Youth service
Barn Dance	

2.   Brainstorm the jobs that need to be done and ask people to volunteer. Ideas might include the following:

Disco organizer
1. Hire hall
2. Book disco
3. Organize bouncers
4. Organize people to clear up
5. Liaise over the refreshments

Treasurer
1. Open account
2. Keep records of all income and expenditure
3. Provide floats for the stalls
4. Bank monies
5. Liaise with Church Treasurer

Leader
1. Organize Insurance

Rock band competition organizer
1. Hire or borrow P.A. equipment and lights
2. If outdoors, stage a wet weather venue
3. Publicity

Publicity
1. Design posters for events and print them.
2. Speak to and give press releases to the local press
3. Speak to local radio
4. Keep the church informed

3.   Start organizing. The event will not happen unless the young people do it. So, as leader, motivate, encourage, support and help them, but try not to do it for them.

4.   The event should be self-financing, with the income from the Disco or Black Tie Ball covering the expenses for the other activities. You could make the event into a charity fundraiser,

by charging stall holders, donating profits, sponsoring the fun run, and then giving the proceeds to a youth charity (another press photo opportunity).

5.   You may need to spend money before you receive income. If your youth group is poor, ask the Church Treasurer for a loan. This is a good opportunity for your Treasurer to talk to the group about how to keep accounts, etc.

Hints

1.   Good publicity and involvement from different sections of the community all help to draw people in.

2.   The event can do wonders for relationships between church and youth group, especially if each young person is linked to a church member.

3.   This is not an activity for predominantly young groups. Some of the tasks will need young people of sixth form age to be organisers, but all ages can be involved on the day.

4.   The process of arranging the day will draw your group together and also give it a much higher profile locally.

Church picnic

Aim

To organize a picnic for church members of all ages.

Preparation

Write four sets of questions (see below).

Equipment

Paper, pencils, telephone access.

Action

1. Suggest the idea to the youth group and divide into four groups to look at the following areas:

Finance
1. What will it cost?
2. Should there be a charge or donation?
3. How could money be raised to cover a loss or to subsidize?

Venue and transport
1. Where shall we go? How long will it take? When to go?
2. How do we get there?
3. How do we let everyone know?

Catering
1. What food and drink should be provided?
2. Who will provide it?
3. When and how will it be prepared.

Activities
1. For everyone.
2. For children.
3. For Dads, for Mums.
4. For oldies.
5. Who will organize each one and the equipment?

2. The groups will need to liaise with each other and then each produce a report, like those below.

Finance
1. Donations only. No charge.
2. Cost for the bus, posters, paper plates, etc.
3. Money to be raised by car washing during morning service.

Venue and transport
1. Trip to local Country Park.
2. Sunday 12 June after 10 am service: return 6 pm.
3. Bus hired for the journey.
4. Notify vicar and church mag., also service sheet.

Catering
1. Bring and share lunch.
2. Youth group to provide paper plates, black sacks for rubbish.
3. Lists to go out at back of church for members to sign.

Activities
1. Singing/rounds, Tag, parachute games.
2. Treasure hunt games, play area.
3. Tug-of-war, races, welly throwing.
4. Nature trail, display area.

3. When the reports have been given to the whole group, discuss the project's feasibility and then, if it looks as if it will work, get the groups to implement it.

Ideas montage

Here are some well known ideas for getting your youth group 'Down the Pole', in case you have never tried them.

1. Baby-sitting

Draw up a list of young people who are willing to baby-sit for church members. Include names, addresses, telephone numbers and availability. Distribute to parents of small children in the congregation. Alternatively, you could appoint a Baby-sitting Co-ordinator to match up sitters and parents. This service could be free or at a fixed fee which is donated to youth group funds. Perhaps you could provide free sitting for parents for church events and a charge for other times.

2. Youth action

Gardening, shopping, reading to the housebound, sweeping leaves . . . Make one Saturday a month a Youth Action Day. Advertise it in the church magazine, the Sunday bulletin or notices, notice board, etc. Members of the congregation can ring in with details of people, places and tasks to be done and then the youth group can spend the day in action. Usually it's great fun, even when the job is a grotty one. It helps the youth group see you the Youth Leader and your Christian faith in practice, instead of theory.

3. Carol singing

Carol singing presents many options. If you are a very small group with no musical talent, why not borrow a couple of musical adults from your worship group or choir?

Instead of singing for money, you could give out invitations to your Christmas services.

You could go to the old people's homes in your area and

lead them in some carols, a Christmas reading and a testimony or short talk by one of your young people.

4. Youth services
These come in various styles and flavours even though the name is dreadful and sounds exclusive (no adults!). These can, however, sometimes be a wonderful opportunity to get your young people involved in the church and expressing their faith.

5. Sleep out
This one is for youth groups with a macho element and whose leaders do not mind hypothermia. So far, I have succeeded in talking our group out of doing this in mid-December. But when summer comes and they want to raise people's awareness of the plight of the homeless, why not sleep out in newspaper and cardboard? Get lots of media coverage and perhaps use this as a sponsored event to raise money for Christians working with the homeless and also to get people involved. Imagine your young people back at school the next Monday morning telling their friends what they did over the weekend and why . . . and the evangelistic opportunities it presents.

Concert
Put on a Christian Concert. Invite a good band and get local youngsters to support. Send the profits to charity.

FAST FOOD FUND
Everyone fasts for one meal a week at school. Give the money to charity.

KIDNAP THE MINISTER
– on a Saturday night or Sunday morning. Ring around, pass the plate or get pledges for Third World as a ransom.

DRAMA FOR THE WORLD
Arrange some street theatre to perform in the local shopping area. N.B. Practise, be loud, be visible, have fun, have leaflets or (1 Peter 3:5) be ready to talk, have a theme.

REDECORATING

RADIO

SCHOOL ASSEMBLY

Car washing

CHRISTMAS TREE REMOVALS

MOTHERING SUNDAY DELIVERY SERVICE
Buy up flowers or raid your gardens. Put them into bunches with labels and deliver to those in church who have no kids to send them some.

ENVIRONMENTAL CLEAN-UP

FASTING
Organize a fast, either:
a. Sponsored, to raise money and awareness.
b. Quietly, with only the group and God knowing. Use it as a time for prayer on a theme, e.g. Evangelism or Revival.

GROUP GROWTH

There is an age-old expression, "It's not what you do but the way that you do it."

This is very true when it comes to group growth. Doing the right activities and holding the right events are unlikely to work until there is an environment for growth.

So what is it that makes a good environment for growth? In some ways youth groups are like plants:

Light	Christ
Warmth	Love, concern, the Father's love
Food	Teaching, action, challenge
Moisture	Spiritual refreshment
Space	To question, grow and investigate
Protection	Safe environment, no bullying, teasing or condemnation

When the atmosphere and basis are right, a group will grow numerically. The speed at which it does so is dependent on three factors: How many members you gain, how many members you lose, and what percentage of the membership attends each week.

How many members you gain
New members are likely to join via a number of different routes:

Moving up from a junior group, Pathfinders, Jucos, etc.

Responding to advertising or information about the group.

By being invited along by members of the group.

For most groups the biggest potential for group growth is through members inviting along their friends.

How many members you lose

Members are lost from the group in opposite ways to how they join:

> Moving up and out of the group – leaving for Polytechnic or University or joining the next group up.
>
> Leaving the area, leaving the group, gaining other interests.
>
> By being pushed out of the group by other members, by being picked on or teased, or because of the break-up of a boyfriend/girlfriend relationship.

What percentage attends each week

If only a small percentage of the membership turns up each week, the first sign of growth will show in regular attendance.

If most of the members turn up each week, the growth of the group will involve drawing in new members.

It is possible to have increasing membership *and* constant attendance. If your youth group is in this situation, you may need to increase the youth participation in the group.

Participation

This means getting the young people involved in the running of the group, letting them make decisions and organize events. One of the best ways of doing this is by having a Members Committee, elected by the youth group. Some of the posts on the committee could be:

Treasurer:	to collect subs, keep records of income and expenditure.
Publicity:	to draw up posters, give information to the local papers, radio and church magazine.
Secretary:	to keep records of attendance, members' names and addresses, the minutes of committee meetings, etc.
Social Secretary:	to arrange social events, liaise with publicity.

Additional posts can be added as the group grows and more areas of participation develop, e.g. Sports Secretary, Prayer Secretary, Church Rep., Worship Secretary, Tuck Shop Manager, etc.

Participation involves risk. There will be costs as well as benefits, for example, the social event that no one comes to, the four boxes of sweets that no one buys. The young people will learn from these failures as well as the successes. Jesus gave His disciples opportunity to do things by themselves and report back what happened. Sometimes they were amazed at what they achieved, at other times they came back with questions.

Developing a fringe
The fringe are the friends, neighbours, school mates and colleagues of the group members, who, though not yet ready to attend the main weekly meeting, will come along readily to sports and social events.

These occasions give opportunity for relationships to develop between the members and the fringe and for you to get to know them. In turn, they have the chance to discover that Christians are not "Halo-wearing Super Saints" or "Hippy Weirdos". The fringe are often the best group to target for special events such as Guest Evenings or Joint Evenings.

As the group grows, so, hopefully, will the fringe. But it is not uncommon for Christian young people to have no non-Christian friends outside the youth group. If you find this is the case, and you still feel that the group needs to grow, then the activities will need to draw unknown people along. You could try a Christmas concert, publicity posters, local radio interview, a what-is-on advertisement, etc.

How big should a group grow?
Jesus' last words were a command to "Go and make disciples . . ." Clearly there is a need for our groups to have an emphasis on outreach. If the group grows too large, how-

ever, more leaders are needed. The quality of relationships decline, individuals get less attention.

A solution to this kind of problem might be to break into sub-groups (cells) and meet on different nights. Alternatively, you could meet for part of the evening programme in small groups and spend the rest of the time in a large group. With this cellular approach there is no limit to growth providing you can find the cell leaders.

New members' draw

Aim

To encourage members to bring their friends along to youth group.

Equipment

A box with a slit in the lid (like a ballot box), a pile of blank cards, two record tokens.

Preparation

Prepare posters for the meeting to explain exactly how the draw works (or get some of the young people to do it).

Action

1. Each time a member brings a person along to a youth meeting, they write the visitor's name, address, age, telephone number, school, etc. on one side of a card and the member's own name on the other.

2. At the end of the term (not necessarily the last meeting) draw one card out of the ballot box and give a record token both to the newcomer and to the one who brought or invited him or her.

3. If either of the young people concerned are not at the meeting, use the record tokens to buy tapes or records for the youth group.

Hints

I used this idea for a year with a youth group in Leicester with very positive results. It helped the young people realize that the Club was somewhere they could invite friends to and the group grew rapidly. Once they had got the idea and the group had grown sufficiently, I stopped using it.

Some may consider it un-Christian to use an inducement or may even call it a bribe. I felt that our Sunday Christian youth programme was of value to all young people, and anything which encouraged the group to invite friends, when peer pressure pushed towards the reverse, would be beneficial.

Doing time

Aim

Warm-up, information gathering, perhaps a new members' guest evening.

Preparation

Forewarn people to come dressed in prisoner or convict style clothes.
Borrow the equipment.
Draw up height chart and code number labels.
Find some volunteers to help with the evening.

Equipment

Polaroid camera and films
Convict Information cards
Ink pad
Height chart

Lunch bags, labels and ties
Standard lamp
Refreshments

Action

1. Divide the space where your group meets into six areas. If you can use six rooms, that would be even better. Label them:
   a) Arrival Area: (where people gather when they arrive.)
   b) Numbering Issue Area: includes confiscation of property. Everyone has to hand in their money, watches, walkmen, etc. Bag, seal and label these and keep safe. Issue each person with a 10 cm × 30 cm strip of paper.

c) Photograph and Height Area: Take a polaroid picture of the person standing against the height chart.

d) Interrogation: Fill in the first section of the convict's information card.

e) Fingerprinting: Take fingerprints on to convict's card.

f) Refreshments: Serve bread and water or char and biscuits.

2. When most people have arrived begin to process them as they pass from one area to another.

3. After everyone has been processed and has had refreshments, do a Bible study on Jeremiah 37: 6–21 or on Paul's imprisonment (Colossians 4:2–10 or Acts). Perhaps end with an appropriate game.

4. Do not forget to return valuables at the end.

Convict's Record Card

CONVICT'S NUMBER: .....
Name ....
Address ....
....
....
....
Telephone ....
School ....
Confirmed ...... Y/N.
Hobbies ....
....
....
Church ....
How long have you been coming to Youth Group? ....
What do you most enjoy? ....
....
What do you least enjoy? ....
....

LEFT	LEFT	LEFT	RIGHT	RIGHT	RIGHT
MIDDLE	INDEX	THUMB	MIDDLE	INDEX	THUMB

Crazy quiz

Aim

To obtain information on a guest night about where people live and what school they go to, etc., without disrupting the flow of the evening.

Equipment

Paper, pencils, score sheet.

Preparation

Write out a list of questions.

How to play

1. Use this activity as part of a number of silly games on a guest evening.

2. Divide into two teams, seated facing each other.

3. Tell the group that you are going to ask questions. Correct written answers will receive points. The team with the most points is the winner and the score will go towards a culminative score for the evening.

4. Count up the final score and declare the winning team. Ask for all the sheets in so you can check the scores. (They will know what you are really up to!)

5. After the meeting, transfer all the names, addresses and telephone numbers to one sheet and send each new person a thank-you card for attending, an invitation card or a programme card.

Questions

1. Have you ever touched a camel?   (Yes 10 pts, No O pt)

2. When were you born?   (person closest to 15 December: 20 pts)

3. Have you ever broken anything?   (Arm 5 pts) (leg 10 pts)   (nose 15 pts)   (wind O pts!!)

4. Do you have a younger brother?   (Yes 10 pts, No 5 pts)

5. Have you ever eaten snails?   (Yes 10 pts, No 5 pts)

6. What is your telephone number?   (1 pt)

7. Do you like cauliflower?   (the team with the most members who do not: 200 pts)

8. What is your full postal address?   (5 pts per word, 10 pts per number)

9.   Do you like maths?   (Yes 1 pt, No 50 pts)

10.   Do you know what a chondrite is?   (Yes 20 pts, No 1 pt)

11.   Have you ever eaten frog's legs?   (Yes 50 pts)

12.   Write your full name?   (20 pts)

Programme cards

Aim

To produce a good programme card. Revised termly, this is one of the best ways of encouraging new members.

Action

1.   Plan your programme with plenty of time to spare before the start of term. This may mean booking minibuses, speakers, hall, groups, etc. much earlier than normal, but it will free you nearer the day.

2.   Outline the programme on paper. Useful information to include might be:
    Where and at what time are the meetings?
    Are there any exceptions to the above?
    What will the social events cost?
    Who do people contact for more details?
    Decide what graphics are to go on the card.

3.   Commercial printing is an expensive way of producing a programme card when just as good a result may be obtained with Letraset and a typewriter, getting your local fast copy shop to photocopy the finished article on to card. A5 or A6 folded cards are good as they fit easily into pockets or Filofaxes. If using folded A6 paper, the result should look as page 158.
    Folded A5 will look like figure on page 159.

4.   When your cards are photocopied, cut and fold them and then they are ready for delivery. Give every member of the group two: one to keep and one to give to a friend. Send one to any members who have fallen by the wayside, to those who

have attended social events in the last few months, and one to any unattached young people at church.

5.   Finally, keep a supply for giving out during the term and also to show adults in the congregation what the youth group is up to.

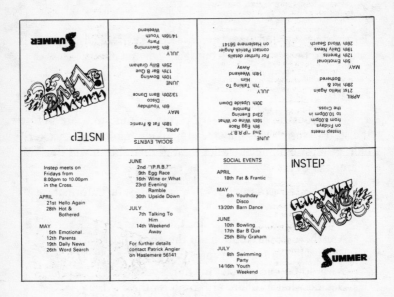

INSTEP

FRIDAY NITE LIVE '88

SUMMER

DATES FOR THE DIARY

MAY   6th   Bring & Share Tea
              (4.00pm Patrick's Flat)

      7th   Charter Fayre
              (We Have A Stall)

      12th   Bowling Portsmouth

      27th   Youth Service 11.15am
              St Stephens

For details of other social events and
the programme for after exam
activities please speak to David or
Sarah or read June Youth News.

SUMMER RESIDENTIAL ACTIVITIES

YOUTH FESTIVAL WEEKEND
Diocesan camp at Boxhill,
13–15th July, Cost £8.00

SUMMER HOUSEPARTY
The Woodhouse Staffordshire
August 26–31, Cost £53.00

Full details in Parental consent letters
or Youth News

INSTEP is the name for all teenagers at
St Stephens the main meeting is with the
rest of the Church family on a Sunday
morning. Instep also meets for its own
activities on a Friday and a Sunday
evening. The Friday evening meeting is
now called Friday Night Live and the
Sunday evening meeting is called S.N.L.F.
Everyone is encouraged to become fully
involved and there are many opportunities
to do so; these include, serving on the
members committee, helping in crèche or
junior church, playing in the Mushite Clan,
serving or cruciferring in church.
If any of these interest you then ask Patrick
or Beverley for more details.

For further details of Instep's activities
please contact Patrick on Haslemere 56141
(home) or Haslemere 56086 (office)

JULY   6th   The Real Thing
      13th   YOUTH FESTIVAL
             (Boxhill Dorking)

APRIL   27th   Starting Up

MAY   4th   Groups
     11th   Taking The Strain
     18th   Route Finding
     25th   Under Construction

JUNE   1st   Solid Ground
     8th   League Champions
     15th   Steve Flashman
          (Joint With 3CS)
          (John Reaney)
     22nd   Cricket vs Vicars 11
          (Meet W. Hill 6.30pm)
     29th   Ice Skating
          (Meet 6.30pm Church)

SUBSCRIPTIONS
Subs are 50p a meeting or £1.00
a month or £10.00 a year

Sports events

Aim

Like social events, sports events are occasions designed not only for the youth group members but also for them to invite friends to, in order to make up numbers. They also serve to unite the group.

Action

1. *Challenge match*. Challenge another youth group to a football, cricket, netball or basketball match – depending on your group's interests. If you do not have enough members, ask the young people to invite friends from school. Encourage everyone to turn up to support. Bring coffee, oranges, etc., for halftime.
– If you are unable to find another youth group to challenge, try challenging the adults from the congregation and perhaps make it an annual event. It is good for relationships between old and young in church, as well as drawing in new members.

2. *Roller hockey*: Hire a sports hall that has both roller skates and unihoc equipment (indoor hockey) and combine the two for a hilarious and fun activity. The object is to play and score goals as in hockey while on roller skates. This has got to be played to be believed!

3. *Bowling league*: If you regularly take your young people Ten Pin bowling, keep the score cards after each game and produce a Youth Group League. Columns could be: number of games, high score, low score, total points, average. Trying

to improve averages or position on the table becomes an incentive for joining in.

4. *Outdoor pursuits*: Arrange a day out. Try climbing, caving, abseiling, canoeing, or sailing. Contract your County Youth Department for details of local facilities and prices. Perhaps ask for the names of instructors if the above are too expensive. If the cost proves to be a problem, why not hold a fundraising event to finance it, or see if local grants are available. (Your denominational youth officer may be able to give you some assistance with this.)

Social events

Aim

To draw members' friends and unattached youth into the church. A good programme of social events can help to build up membership provided each event is integrated into the youth group's general programme and members invite their friends.

Action

1. Hold a Build Your Own Pizza Party. Make up the bases or buy frozen ones, then everyone brings cheeses and different toppings with which to build their pizza. Tomato, mushroom, ham, sardines, olives, sweetcorn, peppers, spicy sausage . . . The varieties are endless! All the toppings are laid out on a table and everyone takes it in turn to build their own pizza. After the pizzas, play some silly games, e.g. spaghetti tying.

2. Go to watch a sporting event – ice hockey, basketball, football, rugby, etc. Book tickets in advance and travel together. It's a great way to get to know the group's friends without their or your realizing it. They in turn will soon discover that lots of their apprehensions about a church youth group were way off line.

3. Try a non-alcoholic cocktail evening. Everyone comes dressed in 1930s prohibition costume. Deck out the youth group hall as a bar and borrow some appropriate music from the record library. Mocktails (as they are called) can taste just as good, and making them is half the fun. You will need a wide range of ingredients. The Band of Hope (45 Great Peter Street, London SW1P 3LT) have a book of recipes for sale.

4. Other good social events are: go-karting, Laser Quest (hunting each other in a space ship with lasers and space wear!), mountain bike racing, barn dances, assault courses, archery, firework party, bring and share meals, boating, day trips . . . and so on.

Hints

Whatever you do, make sure the members do most of the organizing: designing tickets, decorating rooms, deciding times, venues and activities. If they "own" the project it is much more likely to be a success.

Posters

Aim

One reason why young people do not come to youth groups is that they do not know they are happening. Good posters are a way of letting them know about your group.

Action

1. Decide what you would like the posters to say – not just in terms of words, but also in terms of how the information is presented. Style can say as much about the group as the words.

2. Do you have a logo or any graphics that are used on your programme cards, T-shirts, minibus? If so, it would be good to include it somewhere on the poster.

3. Participation! The whole of the youth group needs to be involved in the process, from design through production to dashing around town putting up the posters.

4. For a limited quantity, A3 and A4 photocopies are the cheapest, using black on white or coloured paper. A two-coloured design, e.g. red and black on white, can also be produced by running them through once with a master for the black and then again for the red parts.

5. The group can put completed posters up in school, college, shops, the library or the Sports Centre. Use your imagination – put them wherever young people are likely to see them.

T-shirts

Aim

To produce youth group T-shirts. This is a great group-builder as it gives a strong sense of identity.

Activity

Option 1:

1. Have a Design-A-Logo competition. Everyone thinks up a logo design for the group's T-shirts – one which suits its name and its style. Provide paper, pencils, pens, paint, wax crayons, etc.

2. When everyone has created a design, lay these out on the floor and come to a group consensus on which design or combination of designs would make a good logo.

3. The final design needs to be drawn up, and then either taken to a T-shirt bar to have the design printed professionally, or made into a silk screen print so the group can print their own T-shirts. For the second option you will need to borrow a silk screen and squeegee and then buy inks and stencil films.

4. The advantage of printing your own T-shirts are: the fun, the mess, and the sense of achievement. The disadvantages are the difficulty of printing good quality T-shirts and complex designs.

Option 2:

1. Ask everyone to bring along a T-shirt and a fabric pen or paint. You can provide some yourself, too. Then everyone designs and produces their own T-shirt.

Evangelism

The best way to grow is by the young people in the group reaching out to other young people with the Good News and drawing converts along to youth group. Here are some methods which could be used, either exclusively with young people or with a mixture of young and old.

COFFEE BAR
Why not run a drop-in for non-church youth or have an alcohol-free bar in your hall? Open it late on Friday and Saturday for those who would not come to youth group.

Books

BANQUET
Give out invitations to a free sit-down meal. Mix Christians with non-Christians and let the conversations happen.

MIME

STREET WORK
Instead of inviting young people in – go out to where they meet, in games arcades, bus shelters, fast food take-aways, etc.

DOOR TO DOOR
Traditional method. Always send young people in pairs, preferably two or three pairs visiting the same road. Use a questionnaire or survey to act as discussion starter and information.

EVANGELISTIC CONCERT
Hire a hall and book a Christian band and speaker to preach the Gospel.

Holiday Club

DINNER PARTIES
Four Christian young people invite four non-Christian young people and give a Gospel presentation during the evening, using video, testimony, speaker, etc.,

DRAMA
Short sharp sketches presented on the streets, in youth club, at schools, etc., backed up with the Gospel message.

FOOD

Busking

School assemblies

DANCE

ACT OF WITNESS
Carry a large cross around on Good Friday with prayers, readings, songs, etc.

OUTDOOR ACTIVITIES

What do you do on those warm summer evenings when the daylight lasts until 10 o'clock and the young people are champing at the bit to get outside?

Do you sit them down in front of the latest Christian video, or let them loose on the outside world with an outdoor activity?

Here are a few fun activities if you decide to do the latter. Some are suitable for evening meetings, others for residential weeks or weekends.

Action adventure walk

Aim

Outdoor team building; a fun all-day activity suitable for a week or a weekend away.

Equipment

Maps, compasses and activity equipment.

Preparation

An activity of this kind needs careful preparation and planning. The ingredients depend on where the adventure walk is to be held and the age and capability of the group. Draw up a treasure map based on the house you are staying in during your time away. The treasure is hidden on the site and is marked on the map. Construct the map so that it can be marked up and cut into jigsaw type pieces in such a way that the treasure cannot be found until the puzzle is complete.

Action

1.   Set the scene by giving the group the following information.
   You are about to be dropped in a foreign land in order to recover the long lost and infamous "Lost and not found" treasure map. You are not the only group of treasure seekers looking for the map; your rivals, however, intend to use the treasure for wicked ends . . . When in the foreign country you must not talk to any of the natives; they will recognise your accent and

instantly betray you to the secret police. The roads are regularly patrolled and are best avoided.

2.   Divide the group into teams of five or six members.

3.   Transport the groups by car or minibus and drop them off at a point unknown to them with the following: map, compass, walkman with no tape (optional – see below) and an envelope containing two 10p pieces. Leave them with the first clue:
    Your mission is top secret.
    To find your first target, ring: (give telephone number)

4.   When they ring in, either have someone to receive the call or leave a message on an answer machine. The phone message is:
    The grid reference is: 40652971
    15th December 1984 Mrs. Smith.

5.   At the grid reference given by the phone message is a graveyard and by Mrs Smith's grave is an envelope for each team with their next instructions in it. The envelope also contains a task for the group to do. If the task is completed the team receives as its reward a piece of the treasure map jigsaw and a surprise.

6.   The grid references and clues continue, either as written instructions or even better, if you have time, as tapes that each team listens to on their walkman and then leaves for the next group.

7.   As the groups move around the course, you will need to get a leader to each activity point just as the groups arrive there. This can be done with the same number of leaders as groups providing the activity points are well spaced and the leaders use cars or bikes.

8.   When the groups have reached all the activity points, their last grid reference is for the base where they can put their maps together and find the treasure.

Examples of activities:

1.   Find an item hidden nearby, e.g. a chocolate bar, can of food, fruit cake (Food is always a good incentive and morale booster.)

2.   Retrieve cans of drink from a stream or pond using bamboo canes with string and a nappy pin or hook. Have the "fishing rod" assembled or unassembled, depending on the age and ability of the group.

3.   Solve a puzzle, e.g. assemble a plastic shape into a cube. (There are dozens of commercial ones on the market which only cost about a pound.)

4.   Find lunch, using compass bearing and accurate measurement from an easy landmark, for example: "In the bracken, 100 paces south of the trig point" or "Buried in the sand 25 feet 170° from the No Bathing sign". Lunch should be in biscuit tins or plastic tubs and have to be cooked, e.g. Pot Noodles, Vesta meals, tinned beans, soup, coffee, tea, hot chocolate. These can be heated either on a fire (check it's safe and permitted) or on a tranger.

5.   Break the code. Devise a simple code and use it to write a message which each team has to solve (to their advantage!). The message could read, "Don't forget to ask for the chocolate".

Using a simple alphabet code like this:

A B C D E F G H I J K L M N O P Q R S T U V W X Y Z
Z Y X W V U T S R Q P O N M L K J I H G F E D C B A

the message reads:
WLM'G ULITVG GL ZHP ULI GSV XSLXLOZGV'
Use a level of difficulty in the code which reflects the group's ability.

6.   Disarm the missile. You need the following equipment: bulb holder, baked bean or soup tin, 4.5v torch bulb in a bulb holder, 4.5v battery and three safety pins. The tin is the missile.

To disarm it the group have to light the bulb for ten seconds using only the equipment provided.

7.   Launch a rescue flare. Equipment needed: lemonade bottle full of water, empty lemonade bottle, red paper streamer, reel of sellotape, cork with a hole through it, bicycle pump and connector tube, bicycle valve, assorted bricks and stones. Their task is to launch the red streamer over 10m into the air.

God's smuggler

Aim

Fun, team building exercise for an evening or weekend away. It involves dropping off groups of young people 4 or 5 miles away and they have then to find their way back.

Equipment

Map, compass, torch, instruction sheets.

Preparation

Divide the group into teams of between 4 and 6 (depending on age and ability) and put a leader or junior leader in each group. (If you do not have many leaders, pull in a parent.) Decide if the exercise should be at night or during the day. Collect together the equipment for each group and choose the locations where you will drop the groups. Ask the group to assemble with appropriate footwear and clothing for walking. Brief your junior leaders on their role as foreign clergymen, emphasizing strongly that they are there to ensure the group's safety but not to intervene unless the group is in danger.

Action

Blindfold the group, lead them to waiting cars or minibus and take them to your prearranged destination. When there, read them the following instructions, which you then leave with them.

Instructions:
1. You have been dumped at grid reference. . . .

2. Your task is to smuggle a visiting clergyman to. . . . without being arrested by the State Paramilitary forces.

3. You must observe the following:
    a) The clergyman is a foreigner unable to communicate with the group. (No speaking in tongues!)
    b) All "A" and "B" Class roads are patrolled by State Border Guards: you cannot walk along them, only across them.
    c) The government has formed a number of groups to infiltrate and impersonate smugglers. Do not trust, contact, join any other group which you came across.
    d) All Public Houses have been notified by the Government of expected smuggling and therefore must be avoided at all costs.

Hints

1. Ensure that your leaders (who act as clergymen) keep quiet unless there is a real emergency, however lost, irate, frustrated and furious the young people get.

2. When everyone is back have a hot drink. Then debrief in one of these ways:
    a) Lead a group work exercise. Discuss: Who was the leader? Who was left out? How were the decisions made? Why did you go wrong?
    b) Use the activity as a discussion starter on the work of the international Bible Societies who translate and distribute Scriptures throughout hostile lands.

The dreaded yellow peril pie filling game

Aim

Fun!

Equipment

25 item A's (could be tennis balls, coloured cards, etc.)
25 item B's (could be chocolate money, coloured cards, etc.)
20 water balloons
20 flour bombs
 2 buckets of gunk (yellow pie filling mix is great!)
20 paper cups
 1 large field or wilderness
 1 high powered water pistol for self protection

Preparation

Hide the A and B items around the playing area. Put made-up gunk into buckets, fill balloons with water and make up the flour bombs. Lay out two five-metre diameter circles, perhaps marking them with string and tent pegs. Make one at each end of the playing area (or battle-field!).

Action

Divide the group into two equal teams. Allocate each team a circle as its base and then explain the rules as outlined below. The winners are either the team with the most points, or the team with the least gunk!

Variations

Limitless! Use your imagination and tailor the game to space, numbers and available resources.

Rules

1.   You are Pirates wishing to capture your opposition's island. Before you can attack the enemy, however, you must gather enough money (item B – chocolate money or coloured cards) and then ammunition (item A – tennis balls) to supplement your attack. (Choose appropriate amounts, e.g. 8 units of ammunition and 6 of money.)

2.   When a team has collected this minimum amount, they may trade it in for water balloons and flour bombs.

3.   If a team has managed to gather 11 units of each, however, they may use their secret weapon (the gunk).

Phase 1

1.   You will need one person per team to be Base Monitor, two to be Interceptors, and the rest to be Hunters.

2.   The Base Monitor stays in the circle. (No opposition team member is allowed into the circle.) The Base Monitor counts the items and tells the Hunters what is needed.

3.   The Hunters seek out the ammunition and money and bring them back to base.

4.   The Interceptors try to intercept Hunters of the other team as they return to their circle with their ammo or cash. They intercept by tagging and playing "Paper/Scissors/Stone". Contestants face each other, 1 metre apart, with one hand behind their back. They count to three then bring their hands out in one of three gestures: a fist = stone; flat hand = paper; 2 fingers in cutting motion = scissors.
    The winner is judged thus: Stone beats scissors (as it is used
    to sharpen them)

Scissors beats paper (they cut . . .)

Paper beats stone (paper covers stone)

5. When a team has collected the appropriate number of units, it may enter into the second phase of the game. The other team may not begin phase 2 until all its units have been collected.

Phase 2

1. The Hunters bring to the Game Co-ordinator their money and ammo and these are exchanged for water balloons and flour bombs at an exchange rate of 1 unit ammo = 1 flour bomb, 1 unit money = 1 water bomb.

2. The team then is armed and can attack any member of the opposition except the Base Monitor. They score 50 points for every flour bomb direct hit on an opposition player, and 100 points for every water bomb direct hit.

3. In phase 2, a team may gain extra bonus points by finding more units and these may be traded directly with the Game Coordinator.

4. Bombs of any description may not be taken off opposition players during the game.

Phase 3

1. If a team gets past a required number of units (say, 11 of each), they are rewarded by the gift of some cups and their secret weapon, THE GUNK! The Gunk Bucket, however, must not leave their base circle.

2. Each cupful of gunk thrown over an opposition player scores 10 points. (At this stage you will need to be quick on your feet and well armed to stay "ungunked".)

Phase 4

1. Get cleaned up and count the scores.

Assassin!

Aim

To get people mixing, to learn names and to break up cliques during a residential event.

Preparation

Put the names of all the people present, apart from the Game Organiser, in a circle on a piece of paper. Keep the paper secret at all times

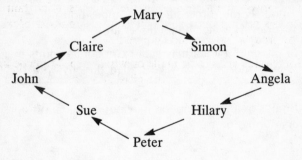

How to play

1.   The game is played throughout a weekend or week away, while the main programme is taking place.

2.   Everyone is an assassin and the object is to be the last person left alive.

3.   Each person comes to the leader to find out who his or her victim will be. For example, Mary has to kill Simon.

4. To kill their victim, they have to get them *alone*, put a hand on their shoulder and tell them that they are dead. A person cannot be killed if there is someone else in the room.

5. When people are killed they are not to tell anyone else that they are dead, nor can they tell the person who they have to kill who has killed them.

6. When Mary has killed Simon (refer to the diagram above), she goes to the game organiser and says that she has completed her assignment. Simon's name is then crossed out of the circle. Mary is now given her next victim's name.

7. Eventually, there are only two left and if they do not succeed in killing each other, the game is a draw.

Hints

1. The order of the names in the circle is important as it encourages mixing between friendship groups and breaks up pairs or groups that are too cliquey.

2. Some rules need to be made on where people can be killed, e.g. boys cannot kill girls in the girls' shower room, etc.

String along

Aim

A simple treasure hunt.

Equipment

Balls of coloured wool, an envelope with instructions inside, a chocolate bar.

Preparation

Cut coloured wool into 10 cm lengths. On the day of the treasure hunt, lay out trails of wool. Tie pieces to plants, fences, gates, bushes, trees, etc. Radiating from the starting point, the trails should lead off in different directions, the pieces of wool being a few metres apart. At the end of the longest trail place the envelope which contains instructions to find the chocolate bar. Place the chocolate bar in the correct position.

Action

1. Tell the young people that the object of the game is to follow the trail to find instructions leading to the treasure. The person who gathers the most pieces of wool will also win a prize. Explain that the trails lead in a number of different directions. The length of time the treasure hunt takes will depend on the length of the trails and how difficult the trails and instructions are.

2. When everyone is back, ask them to count their pieces of wool and give a prize to the person who collected the most (another chocolate bar!).

Treasure trail

Aim

Fun activity to be played in pairs or individually.

Equipment

Pencils, paper, 2 sets of clues.

Preparation

Write out two sets of clues. Put one set in their locations around the neighbourhood. The clues complete a circuit leading back to the starting place. Here is an example:

Location:	*Clue*:
1. Front door of St. Stephen's	A royal Derbyshire valley – if you can notice it.
2. Back of Kingsdale notice board	Haslemere 4552
3. Phone box outside Harding's Post Office.	F Johnson 3 Oct 1917
4. Gravestone close to church back door	Mon to Fri Sat 09.00 09.00 14.15 Noon 17.30
5. At base of post box at Shottermill Post Office	Sat upon by lions

Action

1.   Using the second set of clues give each pair or individual a clue plus a piece of paper and the rules.

2.   When all the teams or individuals understand what they have to do, yell "Go!" and wait for the winner.

Rules
1.   You have all been given different clues.

2.   The first person or pair to complete the course successfully is the winner.

3.   The clues will eventually lead you back to where you started – when you reach the clue you began with, you have finished.

4.   Do not remove any clues.

5.   Please write down each clue in the order you find them so that we know you have completed the course.

Handicap

Aim

To raise awareness of each other's strengths and weaknesses.

Equipment

2 large pairs of headphones (not the little walkman variety), 2 blindfolds, 2 gags, 4 ear plugs, 4 pieces of rope or webbing, 2 maps, 2 compasses, route cards.

Preparation

Plan a suitable course of between 6 to 8km in length, on local footpaths. The route should include stiles, gates, bridges, etc. When you have planned and walked the route, write up a route card for each team. (N.B. The two route cards should describe the route from opposite directions.)

Action

1. Divide the group into two teams including a mixture of ages and abilities.

2. Explain that the two groups are going to walk in opposite ways around the same course and that each team will have a map, compass and route card.

3. Just to make things a little more difficult, each group will have the following handicaps:
    a) 1 person blindfolded.

b) 2 people with their ankles tied together (as for a three-legged race).

c) 1 person with headphones and ear plugs so that he or she cannot hear.

d) 1 person with his or her hands tied behind the back.

4. When everyone has been suitably handicapped in this way, tell them they cannot remove their handicaps and warn them that you will be watching them. Give out the compasses, maps and route cards and let them go.

5. When both groups are back safely, debrief:
What happened?
How did everyone feel at different stages in the exercise?
Who helped who? When and how?
If you could do it again, how would you do it differently?
Would anybody have preferred a different handicap?

6. Conclude in one of these ways:
a) Talking about the importance of working as a team.
b) Discussing how we treat people who are less able than ourselves in one area or another.
c) Discussing how the Body of Christ is made up of different people's gifts and how each is uniquely important.

Egg race

Aim

An outdoor, competitive challenge.

Equipment

Eggs, paper and pens, timing clock with a second hand, instruction sheets and a minimum of two leaders.

Preparation

1.   Make copies of the instruction sheet and give one to each of the teams, a week before the race.

Instruction Sheet

1.   A team consists of three young people.

2.   Each team must choose its own route and provide all its own equipment, including a means of cooking the eggs.

3.   The start and finish point is the church.

4.   When your team is about to start, you will be given three raw eggs to use in the race.

5.   Your task is to race to the Check Point and cook and eat the eggs. (A leader will be at the Check Point to ensure this is done satisfactorily.) Then race back to church.

6.   The winning team is the one whose aggregate time is the shortest (add together the times of all three individuals).

2.   If you want to make it even more fun, why not challenge

other youth groups in the area and send them an entry form, instruction sheets and a challenge poster. (Ask an artistic member of the group to produce one.)

3.   Choose your Check Point. It could be another Church a couple of miles away, a hilltop, someone's garden (someone you know!). The important thing is the distance. It should be 1.5 or 2 miles away, and there must be plenty of different routes to get there.

Action

1.   Send one leader to the Check Point and let all the teams know where it is so that they can plan their route.

2.   Start the teams at 2-minute intervals and await the first arrivals back. As each person returns, write down their time and calculate team times.

3.   The leader at the Check Point must make sure that the eggs are properly cooked before being eaten. (N.B. Try to buy salmonella-free eggs!)

4.   When everyone is back, announce the winners in reverse order and give a suitable prize, e.g. a cream egg each.

5.   Close with an appropriate epilogue. You could talk on the New Life which Jesus brings and "eggsactly" how we can receive it. Don't crack too many egg jokes or else they may become eggsasperated and the yolk will be on you.

6.   Challenge everyone to a rematch next year.

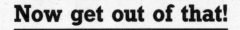

Now get out of that!

Aim

A team work exercise that will involve the group's physical, mental and emotional energy.

Preparation

Careful preparation will ensure that this all goes well. Equipment must be gathered and solutions tested for safety.

Equipment

1 whistle, 1 stopwatch. Other equipment varies with each activity chosen (see below).

Activity 1: Defusing the Bomb

The objective is to remove several small objects (marbles) from the lid of a jam jar. The jam jar is positioned on top of a large tin (or similar) in the middle of a paddling pool full of water.

The paddling pool is surrounded by a 2-metre exclusion zone. This is marked out with string around a radius of 2 metres from the centre of the pool. Warn the group that touching the ground inside the exclusion zone incurs a penalty.

The paddling pool needs to be positioned between two solid trees.

Equipment

1.   One long rope able to take a person's weight and also long enough to go twice between the trees and over the pool with a little to spare.

2.   A teaspoon.

3.   Any other equipment you have to hand, to use as red herrings to confuse the groups as they try to defuse the bomb: 2 garden canes, 2 tennis balls, 1 brick, 1 leather belt, different lengths of coloured string, etc.

Action

1.   Divide the group into teams of five or six. Explain to each team that the task is to defuse the bomb. Explain the rules:

The bomb is defused by removing the four marbles.

A different player must remove each marble.

Nothing can touch the ground inside the exclusion zone. A time penalty will be incurred each time this occurs.

The group may only use the equipment provided, but not all the equipment must be used.

The group has 15 minutes to plan their strategy, during which time they may test the equipment, but no equipment must be assembled when the starting whistle is blown.

The team completing the task in the quickest time wins.

2. When the players understand the rules, the 15 minutes practice time begins. Make sure everything is disassembled when the clock starts for the real attempt. Count the number of times the players tread in the exclusion zone, and replace any marbles which fall into the pool or exclusion zone back into the jam jar lid.

Solution

The task can be completed using a variety of double rope crossings between the two trees along which the team members may crawl, slide, climb and then reach down to remove the marbles using either the teaspoon or their fingers.

Hints

As each team does the activity make sure the other teams are out of sight. Vary the number of marbles depending on the size, age and ability of your group.

Other Activities

1. *Crossing a river*.
Equipment: Larch poles, black plastic drums, string and rope.
Task: To build a bridge which the whole team can cross without any member getting wet. (If there is no canal or river available, mark out a river on a playing field with string.)

2. *Building a raft*.
Equipment: Larch poles, black plastic drums, strings and rope, life jackets.
Task: To travel a fixed distance along a canal or round a buoy in a lake . . . or even up and down a swimming pool!

3. *Lighting a fire*.

Equipment: None.

Task: To light a fire using only what the group can find in the area.

KEEP ON GOING . . .

The rain was blowing horizontal as Henry battled with the church hall door and drips from the broken gutter ran down the back of his neck. Reaching for the lights, he saw tables and chairs scattered from the previous day's rummage sale. Tired and depressed, Henry began to straighten out the mess and set up for the evening's youth meeting. He was prepared this week, having brought a new book of ideas for small youth groups. He had got it all ready, and had even managed a time for prayer.

The hands on the old clock moved slowly around to eight and then to five past, but no one arrived. Finally at ten past, the door opened and Felicity walked in.

"Sorry I'm late, I didn't think it was on tonight, 'til my Mum said. All the rest are at the School Disco – didn't they tell you? It's to raise money for the rainforests."

Henry swallowed, smiled half-heartedly and thanked Felicity for telling him. Then he slowly crumpled up his carefully pre-pared programme and dropped it into the bin on his way into the kitchen and asked: "Do you want some tea? There's nothing special planned for tonight . . ."

One of the hardest questions facing a youth group leader is knowing when to stop and when to keep things going. What began as a joy and a privilege becomes all too easily more of a chore and a problem.

Here are some guidelines which may help.

If you have lost your enthusiasm
This happens to everyone at one time or another, but it doesn't necessarily mean it is time to quit.

When was the last time you met with your minister, pastor or elder to talk about the situation? Never? Or a long time ago? If so, arrange to see him to talk things through.

Have you been on a training course or youth leaders' event, such as a diocesan course, CYFA training weekend or Brainstormers? These are great opportunities to meet others, to be ministered to instead of ministering (remember, if we do not receive as well as give, we dry up), and to learn new ideas and ways to solve problems.

If the group has shrunk to two

The size of the group is no reason for stopping, but it does present problems in choosing activities and planning programmes (see opening chapter). Sometimes when a group has shrunk this small it is better to bring it to an end and then see, after a break, whether God wants it to start again or not.

If the church does not support the work

If the church is not being supportive of the youth work, either in prayer, financially or in the form of personal support for you, the youth leader, it may be time to do something about it. You could get a group together from the church to support you in prayer and fellowship, or raise the issue of the place of young people in the life and worship of the church.

The young people have lost interest

This can happen in a group when the programme gets stale. Even if the programme is good, the young people may become bored with the style and want a change. This can be achieved by a change of leaders or by changing the style of the youth work, for example by increasing participation. However, it is crucial to remember that young people often say they are bored with the group. It is a phase they go through. It is quite likely that you are not doing anything wrong but rather it is their collective mood. Don't give up! Persevere until things change, because they will.

I'm too old . . .

Every age group has different gifts to offer in youth work and youth leaders do not have to be in their twenties. Teenagers relate differently to different age groups and the style of work varies.

I feel guilty when I want to stop

If you have "done your bit", "served your time", then do not feel guilty. As it says in the Parable of the Talents, Jesus will be saying, "Well done, good and faithful servant . . ."

It is usually church members, not God, who make you feel guilty, especially if there is no one to take over from you. Remember, it is God's work and He is responsible for it. If there is no one to take over from you then ultimately you must leave the situation in God's hands.

God calls us to whatever ministries we perform for Him. He empowers us by His Spirit and enables us. The guide for stopping our youth work is the question: "Has God called me into a new ministry?" God guides us through Scripture, prayer, circumstances, other Christians. If God is calling you out of or into youth ministry, then follow His lead.

It takes too much time

Is it the youth group or all the other activities you do in church (creche, housegroup, social committee, bereavement visiting . . .) which takes up all the time? If you want to minister to teens properly, you cannot do all the other church activities as well. That is why Scripture talks about being the Body of Christ. Each person has a different function. If you are trying to do everything, nothing will be done well.

Which of your activities does God say is the number one priority? Do that and ditch the rest. The hardest thing I have had to learn in my Christian life is to say "No" to people. But it is only by doing so that we can be obedient to God's call on our lives.

If you are doing only youth work and it takes up too much

time, it may mean pruning the youth activities or involving the young people in some areas to reduce your load.

Emotions are deceptive

Youth work is a very up-and-down ministry emotionally. Teenagers' moods swing so suddenly and so widely. We can follow the same emotional swings, some meetings being brilliant and others the pits. It is important to be as objective as we can in assessing how things are going.

Reasons for starting and stopping

The reasons for stopping and starting are the same: God calls you. For any ministry to be successful, God has to call, otherwise we are just running in our own strength. "Unless the Lord builds the house, its builders labour in vain" (Psalm 127). When God calls, He also equips for the ministry to which He has called.

So how can you recognize God's call on your life? Here are some ways in which God speaks and some ideas to help you discern what His call is.

God calls through the Bible. Scripture is not only inspired, that is, "God breathed", in its writing, it can also be illuminated by the Holy Spirit in us. Passages can come to life in new and real ways in our personal devotions. When I started feeling called to the ministry, passages kept "leaping out and grabbing me" as the Holy Spirit illuminated them. Personal Bible study is a prerequisite of youth ministry.

God speaks to us in our prayers, as we open ourselves to discern His will. As we listen to the leadings of His Spirit, we can hear His voice guiding us. Furthermore, if we come to God with our fears, needs and anxieties, He is able to heal our fears, meet our needs, and calm our anxieties.

God speaks through other people. We are not Christians in isolation, we are part of the Body of Christ, and the ministries God calls us to are for the building up of that Body. Those in

195

the same fellowship group or house group may discern God's call before we are aware of it. Obviously there is a danger if the church is looking for someone to do the youth work and we happen to fit the stereotype image. But if we are honest with each other and with God in prayer, this danger can be avoided.

God guides through circumstance. Because God is sovereign over all, He can "open some doors and close others" to guide us.

You recognise a need for action. God is a God of action. Part of hearing His call for you to be involved with the young people is your recognition that something needs to be done. Many of the great Christians of the past have been men and women who have responded to the call of God and as they have seen the needs of others around them.

Our task as Christians is to respond to God's call. Just as the fishermen left their nets when Jesus said, "Follow Me," so we should do the same. Our "nets" may mean the housegroup that we lead, or our place in the music group, but the call will be to follow Jesus where He is leading. Similarly, when the time comes, Jesus will call us on into new ministries and the youth work will be left behind.

This may seem a long way from your experience if the Minister asked you to do the Youth Group and you were too scared to say "no". However, God does seem to bless those who honour Him and He will use you and through you bless the group, even if you have not felt His call.

The question to ask then is "Whose youth group is it anyway?" To be successful in the long term a group must belong to God. It must be called by God, empowered by God and demonstrating God's love. However, you have become the Youth Leader, and now is a good time to hand the group over to God and ask Him to be in charge:

Father God,
    It's amazing that you care for this youth group and even more amazing that you love all the members and even me.
    Thank you for demonstrating your love by dying on the cross and bringing us new life.
    I pray that you will take this youth group and its leaders and guide, strengthen and empower us all.
    I pray that your Holy Spirit will make us a true reflection of you and a vehicle to build your kingdom.
    I ask this in the name of Jesus.
    Amen.

Henry sat waiting, crumpled programme carefully ironed, late evening sun casting shadows on the wall. The hands of the old clock had reached five to eight when the door burst open and a gaggle of laughing teenagers entered.

"Hi, Henry, meet Pete and Steve from school, we've been telling everyone how ace Sunday nights are and they've come along."

Soon the room was alive with voices, whispers, giggles and energy as the programme got under way. And somewhere nearby angels were partying . . .